Contents

Introduction 02

Getting Ready 03

- *The work area, tools, materials, and equipment* 03
- *The cloth* 05
- *The (silk) screen* 06
- *Overview of media* 10
- *Design & imagery* 11

Using a Blank Screen 13

Temporary Resists 16

- *Thickened dye* 16
- *Print paste* 19
- *Flour paste* 19
- *Washable P.V.A. glue* 22
- *Masking/decorator's tape* 23

Paper & Plastic Stencils & Resists 25

- *Shredded paper* 25
- *Newspaper & brown paper* 26
- *Freezer paper* 27
- *Book-cover plastic/cover film* 28
- *Tyvek* 29

Fabric-based Stencils 31

- *Painted interfacing: six approaches* 31
- *Painted & cut interfacing* 40
- *Interfacing & fusible web* 42
- *Paper lamination stencils* 44

Semi-Permanent Designs 49

- *Soy wax* 49
- *Drawing fluid & screen filler* 50

Permanent Designs 56

- *Painted acrylic* 56
- *Spray acrylic* 58
- *Webbing spray* 59

Media & Recipes 61

- *Thickened Procion-type Mx dye paints* 61
- *Discharge paste* 67
- *Fabric paints & acrylics* 68

Colour Mixing 70

Re-meshing a Screen 72

Projects: Building Experience 75

Resources/Suppliers 80

Further Reading 81

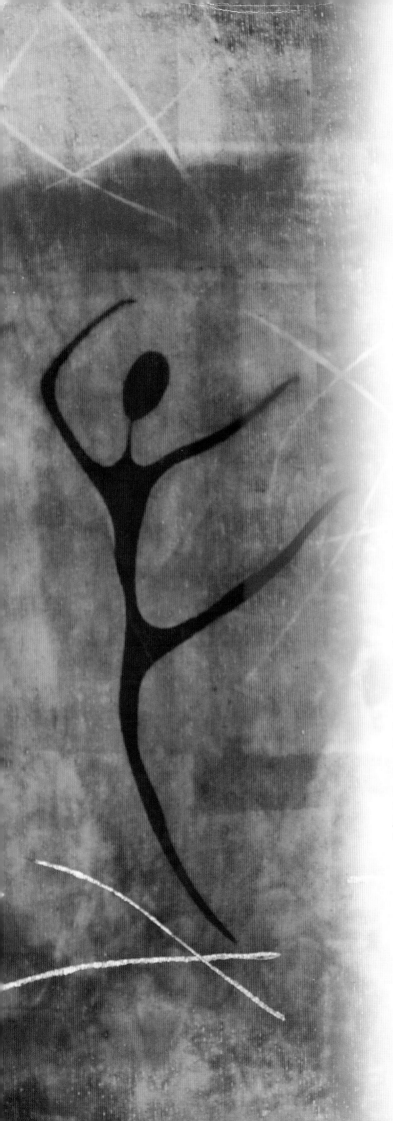

Introduction

Claire was once asked what tool she would choose if restricted to one. A difficult question to answer, but eventually, she decided it would be the (silk)screen – partly on the principle that with a screen, you actually get two tools: the screen itself, and the squeegee.

A silkscreen can be a remarkably versatile tool in the hands of an enquiring mind and an attitude of curiosity. Endless possibilities exist in terms of line, shape and texture. Capable of perfect precision and repeat patterning, the screen can also create marvellously organic, fun and spontaneous results. And there lies the dichotomy: if you're not careful, the 'be perfect' driver can kick in, followed by a somewhat obsessive approach to getting precision prints every time. Be careful of this – whilst at times you may want cloth that has no ghosting, drips or 'dodgy bits', be aware that it is possible to print cloth that seems made by machine, instead of a warm-blooded human being!

At the end of the day, it's all about your intention: what do you want this piece of cloth to look like? What colours, values, textures and imagery do you want it to have? This type of decision-making can be difficult until you've explored the process and got to grips with what it can do. But once you have, we encourage you to start making intentional work: work that is pre-planned and thought through in terms of what you're striving for. And while you're working towards this, be aware that at any stage, a piece of cloth can take on a life of its own and demand to be taken elsewhere; no plan should be so rigid that you ignore what the cloth has to say.

And on that subject, we're not in any way suggesting that you use the silkscreen in isolation. Many of the examples shown in this book have been printed (sometimes as a single layer, sometimes with many layers), but some have also been over-dyed, scraped with thickened dye paint, painted with thin dye paint and so forth. Creating cloth that has complexity and depth will usually mean that you'll use multiple processes or approaches, so think about what's right for each individual piece, don't just reach for the screen because you feel like it.

We suggest you sit comfortably and read the book through from cover to cover. Take a look at the pictures, be inspired and then make a decision as to where to start – which could be anywhere. Just commit to exploring the potential of the screen. You'll be amazed and delighted by what you can achieve.

Getting Ready

THE WORK AREA

The approaches in this book enable you to use a variety of different media. Some are messier than others but if you don't have a studio, a little organisation and planning means you can work in the kitchen, in the dining room, the garden shed, the garage or even a shady spot in the garden.

Wherever you work, setting up the work area is important. If possible, use an area with washable surfaces, or lay down a decorator's cover cloth or a couple of old sheets you can wash and re-use. Worrying about drips and spills will tighten you up. You'll also need an area for wash-up of tools. If you're worried the kitchen sink isn't big enough, a reasonable alternative is a large plastic box parked outside near a drain and filled with water from a hose. Place the box on a small picnic table to make access easier for your body.

Printing Surfaces / Workbenches

If you have to bend too much when painting or printing your back will complain. Ideally, you want the top of your table to be at the height of your pubic bone; about kitchen worktop height – between 85-95 cm/40" – 42". Consider raising your kitchen table on bricks, wooden blocks or pipes. We use plastic plumbers' pipe with a thick piece of wood stuffed inside. The wooden bung is cut to the length the table needs to be raised, then jammed into one end of the wooden pipe. The table legs then slot into the other end of the wooden pipe and sit on the bung, raising the table accordingly.

Our print boards/tables are made from either 9 or 12mm (1/2") MDF or Plywood that can be cut to any size. When considering size, if you're using a kitchen or the garden as a temporary studio, make sure you can lift the board on to a table by yourself. If you're creating a dedicated space/studio, make a print board as large as the space will allow; you'll never regret having a decent-sized work surface to play on.

Cover the plywood with two layers of acrylic or craft felt – stretched and stapled to secure it. Two layers of old blanket or even a layer of old-fashioned carpet underlay/padding is also a good option but either way, avoid a consistency that's too soft/spongy. Suppliers of wide acrylic felt are shown under the Resources section at the back of the book. The print board can be stored behind a wardrobe, under a bed or in the garage/shed – so with a bit of effort, any area can be turned into a studio for a day.

For most of our wet processes we cover the print board with a drop cloth; heavy cotton drill/broadcloth are good options as they're nice and thick and last for ages. An old bed sheet is also okay. The job of the drop cloth is to absorb excess wet media, prevent bleeding and protect your felt covering from becoming damp and contaminated with media. Some of ours have become so magnificent they've been withdrawn from service and turned into storage bags for our work.

Table risers made from plastic pipe and 'bungs' of wood, cut to the required height then slid inside the pipe

Our print boards have two layers of acrylic felt stapled over them. We then cover this with 2 dropcloths

Cloth by Karen Mallik

Tools & Materials

Specific requirements in terms of tools and materials are given for each approach in the book to allow you to select what you need at any given time. Ultimately, you'll be using:

Tools

- 1 to 3 silk screens; waterproofed & pre-cleaned. You can invest in more over a gradual period of time, but 3 are a good starting point. Having them in slightly different sizes/formats can be useful and encourage exploration of scale in imagery.
- A couple of squeegees; one 9"/23cm 'Speedball' type that has a plastic handle and rounded, rubber blade, and a smaller grouting squeegee/ spreader.
- A selection of brushes; a small household paint brush, a couple of artists' brushes (synthetic bristles are fine), a couple of foam brushes.
- A couple of needle-nose bottles.
- A couple of rollers (hard 'Brayer-type' ones, or sponge, or both).
- Items to use as resists (mesh netting, old bits of moulding etc.).
- A craft knife (one with a sharp, pointy blade).
- A cutting mat.
- Scissors (suitable for paper and cloth).
- An iron.

Materials

Specific materials are listed under each approach to allow you to assemble what you need at any given time:
- A roll of 5cm/2" wide masking tape.
- Newspaper and brown wrapping paper.
- A small bagful of paper from your shredder: or simply cut several sheets of paper up into thin strips, then scrumple them up a bit.
- A roll of freezer paper.
- A roll of see-through book-cover plastic/cover film.
- 1 metre/yard (to begin with) of light-weight, sew-in interfacing (e.g. Vilene or Pellon).
- 2 to 3 metres/yards of fusible web, such as Misty Fuse, Fuse FX or similar.
- 1 metre of Tyvek.
- Washable P.V.A. glue.
- A can of Webbing Spray.
- Flour.
- Soy Wax.
- A half-metre/yard of sheer polyester (such as polyester curtaining).
- A pot of basic acrylic paint or household emulsion paint (water-based).
- Fluid matte medium (Golden or Liquitex are good brands).
- A can of temporary, washable basting spray (such as 505).

To print
- A printing surface, covered with the drop cloth, as described on page 3.
- Cloth that's appropriate for the media you're going to use (see notes on pages 10 and 61 to 71).
- Procion-type Mx fibre-reactive dye in a personal selection of colours.
- Chemical Water ingredients (recipe provided on page 63): Urea, water softener and Resist Salt L/Ludigol

- Additive for print paste: sodium alginate (Manutex RS). Recipe provided on page 63.
- Jacquard discharge paste or Formosol powder/crystals for making your own discharge paste (recipe provided on page 69).
- Fabric paints and transparent extender base (information provided on page 68).

Miscellaneous items for screen printing processes & general use
- Several plastic containers – old yoghurt pots are fine
- A lidded plastic container for storing print paste (the size will depend on how much you make)
- A bucket for mixing chemical water, and a lidded container to store it in (plastic water bottles are fine)
- A couple of old spoons
- Measuring spoons (teaspoons and tablespoons are the key measures)
- A measuring jug
- A box of ball-headed or T pins
- A roll of parchment paper
- 2 metres/yards of sturdy sheet plastic

THE CLOTH

We provide more detailed information on fabric choices on page 61, but felt it would be helpful to provide an overview here.

The type of cloth you use will depend on the chosen media, for example:

- *Fibre-reactive Mx thickened dye paints;* Mx dye paints are suitable for all natural fibres except wool.

- *Discharge paste;* will discharge Mx dyed cloth, with the exception of Turquoise which is usually resistant to discharge processes. Commercially dyed black discharge fabric should work, but always test a sample first.

- *Fabric paints;* fabric paints and acrylics will work on any fibre – including synthetics - as they sit on the surface of the cloth and have no chemical reaction to it.

Washing/Scouring the Cloth
Generally speaking, it's best to scour your cloth before using it. Whilst some cloth is supplied 'PFD' (meaning it's prepared for dyeing), others may not be, particularly if bought from retailers or market stalls etc. Scouring removes the size or dressing on the cloth that will prevent dye paints and discharge paste from penetrating the fibres.

To guarantee removal of size, it helps to scour fabric in a rinsing agent such as Synthrapol SP/Metapex 38 and soda ash/sodium carbonate. Textile rinsing agents are designed to remove size from fabric or catch up, hold and remove excess dye from fabric. For scouring with a rinsing agent and Soda Ash, follow the instructions on page 62.

You can make a good start with three screens but if you find you enjoy screen printing, investing in a larger variety of sizes will provide you with flexibility

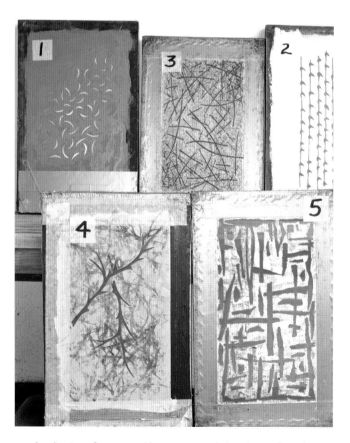

A selection of screens with permanent designs in acrylic paint (see page 57 for instructions)

THE SILK SCREEN - GENERAL INFORMATION & USE

The term silk-screen printing refers to an early phase of the process, when the frame was stretched with silk fabric. Now the mesh is woven polyester. Both wooden and aluminium frames are available. Aluminium is very light but replacing the mesh is almost impossible to do in a domestic studio. A wooden frame is easy to re-mesh using a staple gun.

Commercially produced silk screens feature a mesh that's stretched tightly over the wooden frame by stapling or gluing. Professionally stretched frames usually have a better, tighter stretch than self-stretched ones, but if you ruin a screen, you can get a reasonable stretch yourself (see pages 72-73).

Frames come in variety of sizes – the choice is yours, but remember that very large ones can be difficult to handle when working alone. A useful, easily manageable and easily obtainable size is one measuring approximately 30 × 44cm (12"×17") - measured from the outside edges of the screen. This gives an approximate printable area of 20 × 33cm/8"×13". We have three sizes of screen available in our studio with the following 'inner diameter' (mesh edge to mesh edge) dimensions:

18 × 18 cm (7" × 7")
28 × 28 cm (11" × 11")
34 × 42cm (13.5" × 16.5")

This range provides variety and flexibility and the screens 'nest' inside each other; useful when travelling to teach or study. As you progress through this book you'll see that we refer to the *back* of the screen. The back of the screen is the <u>flat</u> side that is placed against the cloth when you print.

It's important to realize that screens can be damaged or ruined by:

• Polymer-based products such as acrylics, matte mediums or fabric paints that have been allowed to dry on the mesh. Wash out the screen as soon as you've finished using these products.
• Use of inappropriate paints (such as quick-drying ones) or mixing different types of paints that may react with each other, causing an adverse reaction on the mesh, and possibly on the cloth.
• Sharp objects capable of piercing or cutting the mesh.

The left-hand screen is front side up and had been water-proofed with varnish; it therefore needs a masking tape well. The right-hand screen is back side up and had been water-proofed using gaffer tape

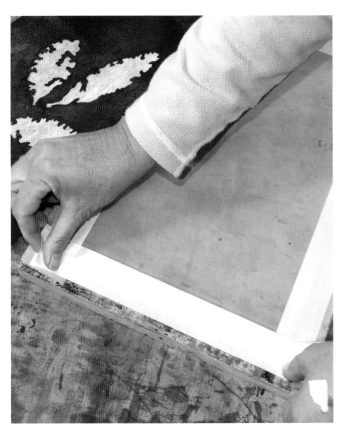

If you've varnished your screens you can create a well using masking tape (torn or straight edge to suit)

Water-proofing the frame

The screen frame needs to be waterproofed before use; otherwise the (usually soft) wood becomes saturated and may warp over time. Proofing screens also means that they can be wiped dry and used again within 10 minutes or so – important if you only have a limited number of screens at your disposal.

There are two approaches to waterproofing the wooden frame:

1. Our preferred approach is to give the wooden frame three coats of water-based acrylic varnish – you'll only have to do it once! Be careful not to drip varnish onto the mesh as it will block the screen during later printing. If you do drip varnish, wipe it off quickly with a damp cloth before it has a chance to set. In case of a real disaster, use 'thinner' and a Q-Tip/rag to rub off the varnish, then wipe down the area with soapy water. Paint thinner is toxic, so don't use it unless you're in a well ventilated place.
2. Another option is to cover the wood with gaffer/water-proof tape (e.g. Duck or 3M), although we find that after a while, the tape has a tendency to lift. If you do use tape, let it 'cure' for 24 hours to achieve a good bond before cleaning or using the screen.

Pre-cleaning the mesh

Whether you buy pre-stretched screens or stretch them yourself, it's always a good idea to clean the mesh after water-proofing the frame. Put the frame under warm running water and scrub the mesh on both sides with a grainy cream cleanser and rinse thoroughly. Dishwashing soap or other cleaners with an oily base are not good for cleaning as they coat the mesh with residue. Towel off the screen, let it sit for 5 to 10 minutes to dry out completely and then you're ready to go.

Creating the 'well'

Some of the approaches in this book require the creation of a 'well'. The well is a blocked-out strip around the perimeter of the screen (about 3cm/1″ wide) where the media is deposited prior to printing. If you've water-proofed the wooden frame with Duck tape, you'll have automatically created a well but if you've varnished it, applying masking tape to the back of the screen is the easy way to create a well. The tape will need to be replaced each time you use the screen as it will lift off during washing, but as taping up takes about 3 minutes, this isn't an issue. Masking tape is also the best tape to use if you want to block part of a screen temporarily. It may bond permanently if left on the screen for long periods of time, so be aware that a 'temporary hold' can become a permanent one.

The Squeegee

The squeegee is the tool used to pull the media across the surface of the screen, forcing it onto the fabric underneath. One of the best is a 9″/23cm blade from Speedball. This squeegee is made with a plastic handle and has a rounded rubber blade that's light, easy to hold and easy to clean. A wooden squeegee with a thick rubber blade is harder to hold and harder to use. If you're printing with small screen, a flat bladed grouting spreader (usually available from DIY/hardware shops) makes a pretty good squeegee. If the squeegee is significantly smaller than the silkscreen, you'll need to do more than one pull across the surface.

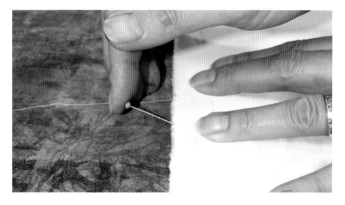

Pinning out the cloth is essential to stop it following the wet silk screen when you pick it up - send the pins right up to their ball heads

A bead of fabric paint is being spooned onto the screen

Here we can see thickened dye paint being pulled from right to left, with the squeegee just off the vertical

As you get to the end of the pull, scoop the media up the side of the screen and deposit it ready for your next pull

Basic Tips on Technique

It's very important to develop competent technique. Whilst there may be occasions where poor technique yields interesting results, perfecting technique is important as it builds confidence and allows you to refine the images you're printing.

- Pin out your cloth: as you pull the wet media across the screen surface it passes through the screen and on to the cloth, which creates the print. When you pick the screen up, the cloth frequently sticks to the screen, so pinning down the cloth before you print is important. Lay out the cloth and send ball-headed pins straight through to the drop cloth and into the felt underneath. Push the pin right up to it's ball-head as then you'll be able to place a screen on top safely. Put the cloth under some tension as you pin it out as it will stretch somewhat as it gets wet with media.
- Whilst screen printing is normally undertaken on dry cloth, working wet-on-wet cloth can yield very interesting results:
    - to work on damp cloth, spin out the excess soda solution in a spin dryer or washing machine, then pin it to your print board on a drop cloth.
    - to work really wet, place sheet plastic on to your print board, squeeze out the excess soda solution then place the wet cloth on to the plastic; use clamps to hold it in place or pin if you don't mind a few tiny holes in the plastic.
- Having organised the fabric, position the screen mesh side (back side) down for your first print; neither in the middle of the cloth, nor on the edge (you'll work off the edges later).
- Position your squeegee in the well – at the top of the screen if pulling towards you, at the right of the screen if you're right-handed, at the left if you're left-handed. **Pulling the squeegee towards you, or from right to left (if right-handed) is the best way to achieve a smooth, even pull... and practise helps too**.
- Spoon/pour the chosen media into the 'well', in a line in front of the positioned squeegee – this is called a **bead**.
- Keep the handle of the squeegee just off the vertical as you pull. Try not to lean it towards you too much as close to upright generates a good print. When you get to the other end of the screen, don't push the squeegee back in the opposite direction. Instead, ease up the pressure and scoop the unused media up the side of the frame and onto the squeegee so you can deposit it back at the top/right hand side of the screen/into the well for continued printing.
- How many **pulls** you need will depend on your own physical strength and the fabric you're using; a fine silk may only need one pull, with fairly light pressure. Heavy cotton may need more pulls with harder pressure. It takes practice to get your print as you want it. As you print, add more media as necessary – the quantity of media is again determined by the design, the cloth and the effect you want.
- Pay attention to the amount of media left in the screen after each pull, and top up as necessary. Position the screen on the cloth and place the squeegee ready to pull for your next print BEFORE you add more media.

The quality of print you get is determined by several variables, either singly or in combination:

- *the fabric type;* fine weights (sheers and light pongees), medium weights (cotton, silk-cotton), heavy weights (felt, heavy cottons/linen). The finer the fabric, the fewer passes required to make a clean print.
- *the wet media;* the consistency of the media has an impact; very thick media requires more pressure. Too watery a consistency results in bleeding and run-off.
- *the pressure you exert;* how hard you press down as you pull the squeegee is directly related to the amount of media deposited on the surface of the cloth.
- *the number of pulls;* generally speaking, between one & three pulls will be sufficient, but since all of the factors are related, it's a good idea to test fabric and wet media before you work on your good-quality cloth.

If you put the screen down on a wet print, the paint will transfer to the back of the screen and then transfer back onto the fabric when you next put the screen down – referred to as a 'ghost image'. This might provide added texture, or create a mess – it depends on what you're trying to achieve. On larger pieces of cloth, ghosting can usually be avoided by keeping the prints apart at the beginning, then going back and printing in the spaces between. If you're printing a close-up, repeat pattern, you can also lay a piece of kitchen towel down over the previous wet print to prevent ghosting, but be careful not to leave it on the wet media (particularly fabric paint) in case it gets permanently stuck there.

Here you can see the 'ghost images' made as a result of putting the screen down on wet prints; sometimes desirable, sometimes not!

When you're printing a whole piece of cloth (as opposed to laying down a single, accent print), try to remember to print right off the edge of the cloth to avoid a 'frame' around the edge. Ultimately, you need to practise on different fabric types and with different media in order to understand the variables and gain some level of proficiency in using them.

You can prevent ghosting by covering wet prints with kitchen towel

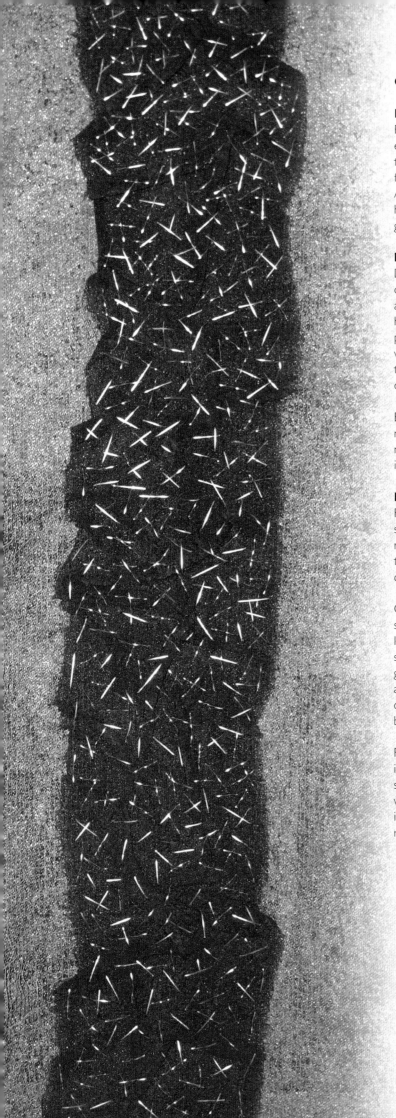

OVERVIEW OF MEDIA

Procion-Type, Fibre-Reactive Mx Dye Paints

Fibre-reactive Mx dyes are suitable for all natural-fibre fabrics except wool. They are mixed with several ingredients to transform them into paints and need a chemical additive in the form of Sodium Carbonate (commonly referred to as Soda Ash) in order to bond with the fibre and fix permanently. A huge range of colours is available, and guidance and recipes are given on pages 61 to 66.

Discharge Paste

Discharging agents are used to remove colour from cloth. Most of the off-the-shelf products (such as Jacquard Discharge Paste) are formulated to remove colour from Mx dyed fabric. Whilst we have used Jacquard, we now prefer to make our own discharge paste using a chemical called Formosol. It's mixed in a little warm water and then added to the same print paste used for making thickened dyes. More detailed information and recipes are given on page 67.

Black commercial fabrics will often discharge – some are manufactured specifically as dischargeable fabrics. However, not every piece of black cloth you buy will discharge, so it's important to test it first before buying an entire roll!

Fabric Paints & Acrylics

Fabric paints sit with the acrylic family, but are manufactured specifically for use with fabric, rather than paper. Drying retardants and surfactants (wetting agents) are usually added to them and a good fabric paint should not alter the hand of cloth in the same manner as an acrylic paint.

One key advantage of fabric paints is that they sit on the surface of the cloth and don't require chemicals to fix them. Instead, they are bonded to the surface of the cloth by heat-setting with a dry iron. Another advantage is that they are generally very light-fast. A huge range of ready-mixed colours are available in both transparent and opaque hues, and you can also opt to buy pigment and mix it into a polymer fabric binder or transparent base extender.

Fabric paints are easy to use but they must not be left to dry out in a silkscreen, or on any of your tools. If they do, they will seal the screen mesh or stiffen/glue together brush bristles permanently, so wash up the second you finish working with them. More detailed information and guidance on use is given on page 69, but always read the manufacturers' instructions carefully.

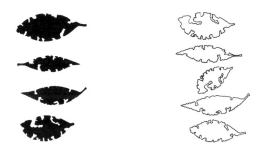

Two leaf designs: one will provide shape, the other will provide outline

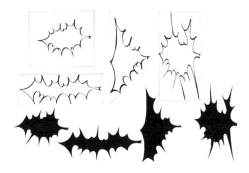

Here we see the result of the abstraction exercise in '**Finding Your Own Visual Language**'. Leslie has developed these designs further and used them in her work (see pages 31 and 75)

The stencil on the left will print a positive image, the one on the right will print a negative image

The image on the right was (accidentally) created when the ink leached through on to a second piece of paper. Serendipity!

DESIGN & IMAGERY

What designs will you make with the approaches in this book? How do you want your cloth to look? Difficult questions to answer when you're starting out.

One key thing to remember is that it's rare for a piece of cloth to succeed as whole cloth after a single process. On the other hand, cloth that's destined to be cut up and re-structured (as in quilt-making) can hit the mark after one process. Compositional cloth will often need between three and eight layers of process to become complete, so bear this in mind and don't get too judgemental after process one!

Some key pointers include:

• *Contrast and relationship;* building contrasts and driving relationships within any piece of cloth will add visual interest. Perspective is worth determining in advance - what is background and what is foreground?

• *Colour;* subtle continuations and build-ups of existing colour: working in a close colour range or in a monochromatic theme: colour contrasts (from the subtle to the flagrant). Colour use is important.

• *Value;* varying one colour from light to dark to create shadows and movement.

• *Transparency;* use very sheer dye paint mixtures or transparent fabric paints to achieve delicacy and to allow underlying colours and imagery to gleam through. Discharge can also achieve this for you.

• *Opacity;* use opaque fabric paints to generate contrast, to drive up impact and to emphasise a sense of an image being 'on top' or obviously foreground.

• *Imagery,* what addition will move the piece forward? Think line, texture and shape. Relationship is key.

• *Scale;* what size imagery works best? Do you need to include a range of different sizes of mark? This is particularly important if you're trying to develop a sense of perspective.

The approaches covered in this book will allow you to create designs in both positive and negative images, and we've provided examples of both as it can take a bit of practise to get your head around this.

The photographs share ideas explored in our studio. Review, contemplate, make some decisions, and get cracking! If you're interested in developing your own personal imagery, or learning about composition in more depth, you may want to consider investing in one of our other books – '**Finding Your Own Visual Language; a practical guide to design & composition**' – co-authored with Jane Dunnewold.

Using a Blank Screen for Colour, Value & Texture

A silkscreen - just as it is — is capable of generating a fabulous range of colour, value and texture. When using a blank screen, acknowledge that you'll be printing the shape of the screen; either a square or a rectangle.

- Media: choose the media you're going to use - thickened Mx dye paints, discharge past or fabric paint. DO NOT use different media at the same time.

- Cloth; choose cloth appropriate to your plans and the media and make sure it's been scoured (and soda soaked if using Mx dye paints).

- If the cloth is dry or damp, lay a drop cloth on to the print table and pin it down. If wet, lay it on plastic and use clamps or pins (see notes on page 8).

- Create a well if you want one —although it's not a prerequisite to this approach.

- Place the silkscreen on to the cloth (not dead-centre and not at one corner).

- Place the squeegee at the top end of the screen and rest it against the edge of the frame.

- Add a bead of your chosen media edge-to-edge across the screen, just in front of the squeegee, then pull it smoothly and evenly across the screen, keeping the squeegee just off the vertical.

- You'll be printing the shape of the screen (a square or a rectangle). Keep printing, making sure you overlap prints (unless you want some white space).

- It can be interesting to print two to three layers, and you may wish to consider changing the size of the screen at some stage.

Christine Chester uses a blank screen as a start to creating background

Printing in progress; initial prints have been laid down with turquoise before switching to golden yellow. The green prints occurred when the residue turquoise dye in the screen contaminated the golden yellow

Further along with the same blank screen: over-printing is now taking place

String has been looped around the pins securing the cloth to the table to act as a resist. A blank screen is being used to print thickened brown dye

Scrumpled cloth being loosley pinned prior to printing with a blank screen

Variables with a blank screen include:

1. Use print paste to weaken the strength of the dye paint and print a layer all over the cloth. Now print a second layer using a stronger value of dye paint. Now print a third layer using your strongest value of dye paint. Keep looking and give consideration as to placement as you progress.

2. Use print paste to weaken the strength of Discharge Paste and proceed as above.

3. In a similar manner, you can increase the transparency of your fabric paint with Extender Base/Binder.

4. Try placing a bead of clear print paste on to the screen, then add dribbles of dye or discharge paste on top of it. Pull the mixture across the screen; you can create gorgeous streaky effects.

5. Use more than one colour at a time in the screen.

6. Place temporary resists such as leaves, bits of thread, sticky mesh tapes etc. on to the cloth. Place the blank screen on top. Pull your chosen media across; usually, the resists will attach themselves to the screen. If so, just keep printing. If not, re-position the resists with every print. Acknowledge that resists will generate a negative image (more on this approach later). If re-positioning them, consider turning them over so that any dye or paint is deposited on to the cloth on the next print, creating a positive image; this is a particularly fun thing to do when you're using different colours.

7. If your cloth is pinned out, create linear marks by looping thread or ribbon around the ball heads of the pins; back and forth in grids or zigzags across the cloth. You'll create linear or grid line effects in the negative image when you print on top of them, as they'll resist the media.

8. Don't pin the cloth out before printing. Instead, scrumple it up loosely (but artfully), make a print, re-arrange/re-scrumple it, print again, re-arrange/re-scrumple. Keep doing this until your satisfied – this approach can generate shard-like effects.

When finished, process your cloth accordingly and rinse as necessary (refer to the specific instructions for each type of media on pages 61 to 69).

You can also use a blank screen as a monoprinting 'plate'. The technique is very simple, but only use thickened dye or discharge paste for this approach, as fabric paints tend to dry out too quickly and seal the mesh:

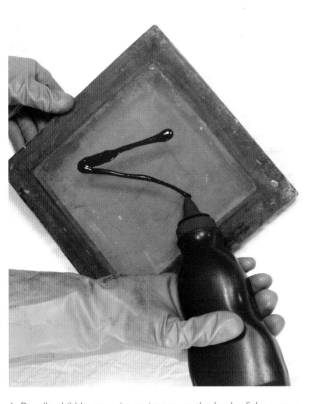

1. *Doodle, dribble or squirt an image on the back of the screen.*
2. *Gently touch the cloth with the screen; the wet media will transfer itself.*

4. *Apply more media to the back of the screen and repeat the process until you're satisfied - you'll get a lot of ghosting and additional texture with this approach, but the results are often fantastic.*

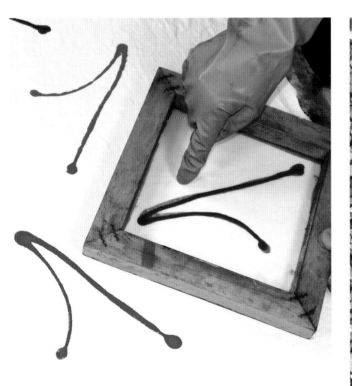

3. *Now place the screen on to the cloth a second time. Press harder and more paint will transfer itself.*

5. *When you're finished, don't wash the screen. Instead. Leave it suspended on a litter tray or towel to dry out, face up.*
6. *Then, use it for an approach called 'Breakdown Printing', which is covered in the next section.*

Temporary Resists

Using temporary resists on the back of the screen is a great way of exploring imagery, colour and texture and we've covered six key methods – although once you get going, you may invent/discover more of your own.

THICKENED DYE

Using thickened dye paint and/or print paste directly on the back of the screen is a wonderful process. It has many variables, all of which are covered in one of our books, '***Breakdown Printing – New Dimensions in Texture & Colour***'. However, it's an approach that can't be ignored in this book, so read on to find out more about the basic principle…

Simply put, thick dye paint or print paste is applied to the back of the screen, left to dry and then printed off. **There is only one rule; only use dye paints or clear print paste on the screen. Do not use fabric paints – if left to dry on the screen, they will seal the mesh – in which case, you'll have inadvertently leapt to the approach covered on pages 58 to 59.**

This approach initially generates *negative* images, which can gradually evolve into *positive* images, with a delicate line around the edges.

Prepare the screen:
- Assemble your chosen colour range of thickened dyes in squeeze bottles.
- If you want to, create a well on the back of the screen by using torn or straight-edge masking tape.
- Dribble, doodle, draw or write on to the back of the screen in your chosen colours of thickened dye paint. Acknowledge that the paint will spread as it settles in to the mesh, so take this into account.
- Place the screen flat on newspaper, a litter tray or a drop cloth to dry as some dye will inevitably drip through the mesh. If possible, put the screen somewhere warm to dry out completely (this is a great process for sunny days). *Note;* the dye-paint resist will take longer to 'breakdown' if the painted screen is left overnight or for a couple of days.
- The applied dye paint will initially act as a resist, so to begin with, you'll be printing in the negative image (the design will be white, or the colour of the cloth you start with).
- Once the dye is completely dry, you're ready to print…

A breakdown screen made by Jan Wise by doodling with thickened dye; the dye must be dry before printing off

Printing

1. *Pin out dry, pre-soda'd cloth (un-dyed or pre-dyed).*

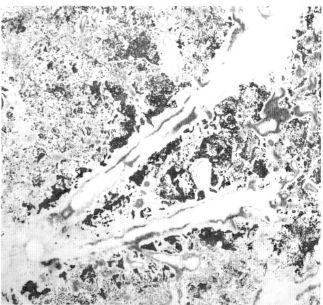

2. *Lay the screen down on your cloth and spoon in a bead of clear print paste, then add a bead of dye paint on top of it. Or just start printing with your dye paint and no added print paste.*
3. *Pull the paste across the screen. The doodles of dry, thickened dye will act as a resist; so you'll get a negative image.*

5. *Eventually, the doodles of dye will cease to resist; they'll start to leave a faint halo of colour in the positive image, often with a delicate, fine, sharp edge to them. Eventually, they'll transfer off the screen, on to your cloth. Leave them there.*
6. *If you want a radical change of colour at any stage, scoop the excess media out of the screen with the squeegee and deposit in a cat litter tray for re-use. Then add the next colour of choice to the screen.*

4. *Lift up the screen, re-position and continue printing. Experiment with using different colours and/or adding clear print paste to the mix. In this image, we're printing with the screen we used for monoprinting on page 15. It was left to dry in order to then breakdown print with it.*

This process offers endless opportunities, so do experiment with the following options;
- print on white or pre-dyed cloth
- print with one or several prepared screens
- print sections of the screen, rather than all of the screen
- leave prints independent of each other, or over-print
- print with a prepared screen, and use a blank screen to over-print or lay down solid'ish areas of colour

And so on.

*Clear print paste has been doodled
on to the screen and left to dry*

PRINT PASTE

As an alternative, you can apply clear print paste to the back of the screen in the same manner as described with thickened dye paints. Once the print paste has been applied, leave the screen to dry (the print paste will take longer to dry than dye paint). Then either…

- Print off using dye paint; this will give clear areas of negative imagery and you can vary colour and value by using dye paints on their own, or combing them with print paste.

OR

- Print off using discharge paste; print the screen using discharge paste on a medium-to-dark value piece of cloth. For discharge paste, remember that the cloth doesn't need to be soda-soaked. When you've finished printing, process the discharge paste as outlined on page 67. Then rinse your cloth well to get rid of residue paste.

We'll now move on to explore eight other temporary resists. All of them can be used with any media; thickened Mx dye paints, discharge paste or fabric paint. **When using fabric paints, wash the screen immediately and get rid of any remaining resist.** The paint can sometimes try to bond with the resist and set permanently. When using thickened dye paints or discharge pastes, the screen can be left and re-used (assuming the resist is still holding up).

When re-using a dried out resist screen, start by placing it on an old towel. Mist it with water and draw a squeegee across it a few time; this will clean it up and release any dried dye paint or discharge paste from the mesh.

FLOUR PASTE

Flour paste can be applied in a thin layer across the back of the screen and left to dry. Marks are then etched in to it to create positive imagery. To make the paste, use the following recipe:

1. *Mix together approximately equal parts of flour to cold water (e.g. 200g flour to 200ml water); the amount depends on how thick you want the paste to be – experiment with different consistencies. We find that a consistency of thick, slightly runny honey works well.*

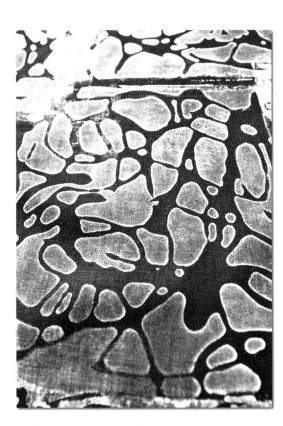

Black cloth printed using the breakdown approach with discharge paste

2. *Drift the flour into the bowl of cold water and beat with an electric stick mixer.*
3. *Use the paste immediately – any leftovers will need to be covered, refrigerated and used within about 2 days.*

To create the design:

1. *Place the screen on a piece of plastic or newspaper, mesh side up.*
2. *Lay a fat bead of flour paste at one end – use plenty, you don't want to run out!*

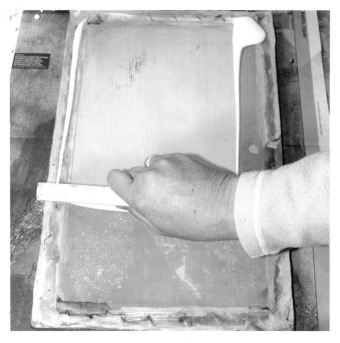

3. *Use a squeegee to draw the bead of paste smoothly and fairly quickly from one side of the screen to the other; aim for a thin, even coating. Don't attempt to scoop up the excess on to the squeegee, just pull right off the edge of the screen and deposit the residue on to the table.*
4. *Leave the screen to dry flat.*
5. *Scoop any unused flour paste back into the pot. Covered and refrigerated, it will keep for a day or two. Then clean up.*

6. *When the flour-paste coating is completely dry, use a wooden skewer to carefully scratch out a design/imagery; be careful you don't pierce the mesh as you scratch.*

A portrait has been scratched out on a flour paste screen by Karen Mallik

To print:

Choose appropriate cloth and prepare it accordingly (e.g. if using dye paints, soda soak and dry the cloth first). For this approach, always work on dry cloth as working wet-on-wet will speed up the deterioration of the screen.

- Print the screen using thick dye paint, discharge paste or fabric paint. The media will come through the scratched out areas, as a *positive* image but won't (initially) penetrate the flour paste. Eventually, the flour paste will break down, but you should get many prints before this starts to happen.
- Be careful when using fabric paints; watch that they're not drying out in the screen and clogging the mesh.
- When you've finished and/or the design has broken down completely, wash any last bits of flour paste residue off the screen using hot water and a brush. If the flour paste proves stubborn, let the screen soak in some hot water for an hour or so and then scrub using a cream cleanser.
- Process the cloth according to the media used (see specific guidance on pages 61 to 69).

The resulting discharge print being activated with a steam iron

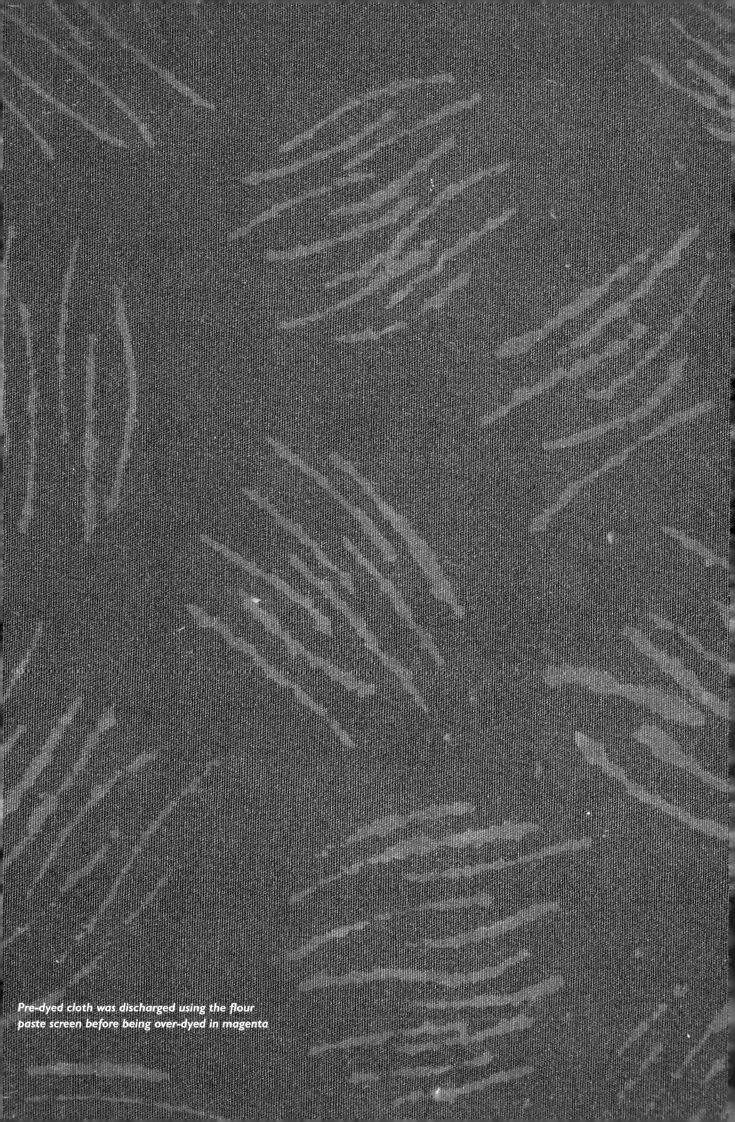

Pre-dyed cloth was discharged using the flour paste screen before being over-dyed in magenta

WASHABLE P.V.A. GLUE

Washable P.V.A. or 'school glue is an excellent temporary resist on a silkscreen and can be bought from craft shops, art stores or places such as The Early Learning Centre. Always test them first by applying some to a small piece of cloth, letting it dry then washing it out in warm to hot water. This type of glue should not be thinned with water, as it will weaken the resist qualities. The designs you create will be *negative* images.

• *Place your screen flat on newspaper or a washable surface, mesh side up. Create a well and/or alter the shape by using book cover film (see page 28)*

• *Apply the glue in almost any manner you like; doodle, sketch, write, smear. Leave it to thoroughly dry (this may mean over night). Remember that the glue will resist the media and therefore print a negative image.*
• When the screen is printed, the P.V.A. will slowly break down, which has a couple of implications:

   - Fixing printed thickened dye paints will not cause the transferred glue to set permanently in the cloth, so these are the safest option to use.
   - If using discharge paste or fabric paints, test a sample first as the glue that's transferred to the cloth during printing may fix permanently when you steam iron the discharge paste to activate it, or heat set the fabric paint.

• Whatever media you use, you'll need to rinse the cloth after processing the media appropriately. This will wash out any glue residue deposited on the cloth. If the glue proves stubborn, soak the screen in hot water then scrub the mesh with a cream cleanser.

MASKING/DECORATOR'S TAPE

Masking tape/decorator's is perfect for creating all manner of negative imagery on a screen. As you build the design, it can help to hold the screen in front of a dark background from time to time – squint at it and focus on the dark areas where there's no tape; this is what will print.

- **Create a well;** *start by making a well. For a torn masking tape design, tear 2 strips of 5cm/2" wide masking tape off the roll, long enough to match the length and width of the screen. Tear each strip in half lengthwise to create 4 strips and apply them along the join between the wooden frame and the mesh. For a straight-edge well, just apply strips of tape off the roll.*

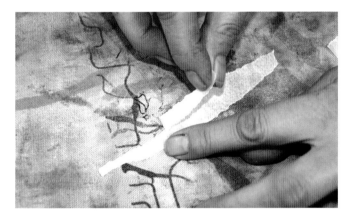

- **Torn edge;** *torn masking tape provides a lovely, rough organic edge to a line. Tear it into strips and/or shapes of different sizes and stick them to the back of the screen; if the pieces are very small, they may fall off during the printing process, but we tend to view this as a serendipitous element of the design process!*

- **Cut edge;** *masking tape comes in many widths. Quarter inch masking tape can be laid down in lines and grids, whilst wider masking tape can be used to cut out shapes.*

- **Bendy tape;** *some hardware shops sell bendy masking tape that can shape gentle curves. If you can find this, give it a go.*

Screens made with masking tape can be printed with thickened dye paints, discharge paste or fabric paints. To print:

- Select cloth appropriate to your media (and if using thickened dye paints, make sure it's soda-soaked).
- Pin or clamp it to the covered print surface if dry or damp. If wet, lay down plastic first.
- When finished either:

  - Wash the screen thoroughly and remove the tape (use a catcher in the plug to prevent little bits clogging up your pipes), or...
  - If using dye paints or discharge paste, you have the option to wipe the screen out using a damp cloth and returning to it later.
  - If you've been using fabric paint, always wash the screen immediately and remove the tape as paint residue can get stuck underneath it and may seal the mesh permanently.
  - *Note:* if the tape has been on the screen for several days, glue residue may transfer from the tape to the mesh. If this happens, soak the screen in some hot water before scrubbing the mesh with a cream cleanser.

- Process the fabric according to the media.

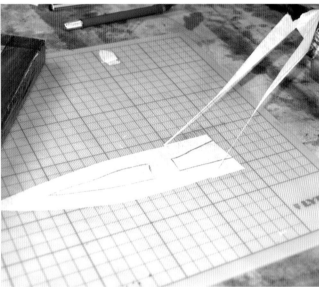

Cutting letter forms from masking tape.

Printing with the cut masking tape screen; remember that your letters and words will get reversed (AAAH becomes HAAA).

Paper & Plastic Stencils/Resists

There are several paper and plastic materials available to create a temporary stencil or resist on the screen. Some allow you to create precise imagery, others are more organic and spontaneous.

Shredded Paper

Leslie and I watched a friend – Leslie Jenison – scatter paper scraps from her shredder on to her cloth and then use a blank screen to print over it. The results were stunning. With this approach, you'll generate *negative* imagery.

- Select your cloth and prepare it accordingly.
- Pin it to the print surface (this process works most effectively on dry cloth).
- Scatter a few handfuls of shredded paper over the cloth; you can be completely random about this and scatter all over the cloth, or scatter an area equivalent to the size of screen you're using. Try both approaches as the results are different. If you don't have a shredder, stack several sheets of paper together, place them on a cutting mat and attack them with a rotary cutter.
- Remember that the paper will act as a resist, and you'll therefore be working in the *negative* image.
- Use a blank screen to print your chosen media; you'll find that some of the paper will attach itself to the wet screen and become a temporary resist on the screen itself.
- As you print, you may need to rearrange the paper or remove some. Pay attention as you work and make decisions.
- When you've finished, use a squeegee to scrape off any paper stuck to the screen and dispose of it, then wash the screen. If you're using fabric paints, do this quickly as the paper and paint may try to bond to the mesh.
- *Dye paints:* you can leave paper on your cloth as it dries, then pick it off before batching.
- *Discharge paste:* again, you can leave bits of paper on your cloth whilst it dries, and pick it off before activating the discharge paste with a steam iron.
- *Fabric paints:* having washed your screen, it's advisable to remove the paper scraps from your cloth before the paint dries as it may bond to the fabric (which may be desirable at times, but not always what you had in mind!).
- Process your cloth according to the media used.

You can see the shredded paper under the screen. Print paste and dye paint are being poured into the blank screen, just in front of the squeegee

The shredded paper acts as a resist to create negative imagery

The resulting piece of cloth. (You'll see it again later, over-printed with fabric paint)

Newspaper & Brown Paper

Most of us have plenty of newspaper sitting in the recycling bin, and you can use brown wrapping paper for this approach too – it's slightly more durable than newspaper.

1. Cut a piece of newspaper or brown paper about 1cm larger than the mesh area of your screen.
2. Tear or cut out your design. Positive imagery: you'll use the sheet of paper with the shape cut out of it. Negative imagery: cut shapes from paper and use them as resists (this approach is illustrated in the photographs).
3. Pin your prepared cloth out on to the print bench; dry cloth works better than wet with this approach.
4. Make a well on your screen from masking tape.
5. Place the paper stencil where you want your first print.

7. This first print will wet the paper with media, causing it to stick to the back of the screen and come off the cloth.
8. Continue printing: as the paper becomes more and more saturated, it'll start to break down or tear and may eventually may fall off the screen entirely – at which point it's time to start again. This 'deconstruction' can be very useful and freeing.
9. If you're printing with fabric paints, the paint that gets on to the back of a newspaper stencil is likely to ghost – often pulling off the print from the newspaper and adding it to your cloth, which can be delightful.
10. When finished, remove the stencil from the screen (if it hasn't already fallen off) and wash up.
11. Process your cloth according to the media used.

6. Place the screen on top of the stencil and make the first print with thickened dye paint, discharge paste or fabric paint.

Figures printed with a paper stencil

Freezer Paper

The silicone coating on freezer paper is often used to iron on a stencil or resist directly to cloth. It also provides an excellent, temporary bond when ironed on to screen mesh. It's a very good option for creating fiddly, delicate designs and you can choose to work in the *positive or negative* image.

1. Cut the freezer paper about 1cm larger than the mesh size of the screen.
2. Draw a line approximately 5cm/2" inside the outer perimeter: this provides a frame to work within.
- **Tip:** to prevent the freezer paper from curling as you cut/tear, place it silicone (shiny) side down on to baking parchment and run an iron (set to wool) over it a few times (no steam).
3. The silicone side of the paper will be the side placed on to the back of the screen. Make sure you work silicone side up when cutting or tearing, otherwise your design will be reversed.
4. Cut or tear out your designs to print positive images. If cutting, use scissors or tape the freezer paper to a cutting mat, silicone (shiny) side up and use a craft knife. Consider saving the pieces you cut or tear out for use as negative imagery.

7. Turn the screen over and place a pad (an old towel will do) inside the wooden frame in a manner that supports the mesh.
8. Continue to iron the stencil. Work steadily back and forth across the freezer paper – again, keep the iron moving so the heat doesn't scorch/catch the polyester mesh. If nervous, place parchment paper on top of the stencil first.

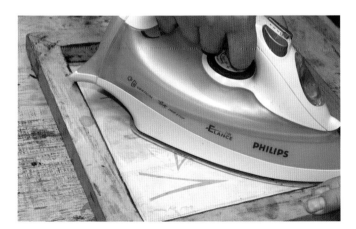

5. Now place the freezer paper stencil silicone side up on the print table. Place a screen on top of it, with the mesh against the freezer paper.
6. Using an iron set between wool and cotton (no steam), start ironing the mesh; the heat will cause the silicone to stick to the mesh. Work quickly and smoothly as you don't want to burn or melt the polyester mesh. If you're nervous about this put parchment paper over the stencil. Don't try to get a good bond all round – it's difficult to get the iron right into the corners of the screen, instead…

9. Finally, tape down the edges of the stencil to prevent any leakage when printing.
10. If working in the negative image, create a well on the back of the screen, then place your torn or cut pieces of freezer paper on top of the back of the screen, cover with parchment and iron down. With complex designs, you may need to iron on the freezer paper one piece at a time.

To print, pin or clamp down your prepared cloth. Use thickened dye paints, discharge paste or fabric paints and process your cloth according to the media used.

Cover film is best used for simple imagery such as these rectangles

Peel off the paper backing and take the screen to the cover film, NOT the film to the screen

Cloth printed with a cover film stencil; one side has been over-printed and if you continued to do a lot of over-printing, you'd create marvellous texture

Book-Cover Plastic/Cover Film

Book-cover plastic or cover film is available from most stationery stores and is a good material for stencils. Good for clean, sharp edges but when considering your design, be aware that at some stage, you'll have to peel off the backing paper. As such, we recommend that cover film is best used for simple, shape-based designs. You can work with *positive or negative* images with this approach.

- To generate a *positive* image, cut out a piece of sticky-backed plastic about 1cm larger than the mesh area of your screen.
- Draw a line approximately 5cm/2'' inside the outer perimeter: this provides a frame and will ensure your design doesn't go outside of the printable area of the screen.
- If you wish to, draw or trace your designs on the paper-side of the cover film.
- Place the cover film paper-side up on to a cutting mat, and anchor the four corners with masking tape.
- Carefully cut around the motifs/marks with a cutting knife (keep the cut-outs if you want them for negative imagery). What you cut is what you'll print – you're working in the *positive* image.
- Remove the masking tape from the four corners and carefully peel off the protective layer of paper, leaving the stencil flat on the cutting mat, sticky-side side up. Do not attempt to pick up the stencil, instead…
- Carefully position the back of the screen over the stencil; look carefully to make sure it's properly positioned in terms of the design. Then, lower the screen on to the stencil and using a squeegee, press down to attach it firmly.
- Pick up the screen and flip it over – the stencil will be stuck to the screen mesh; you can get rid of any small air bubbles by burnishing with a spoon. Apply masking tape along the wooden edges of the screen, over and on to the cover film stencil; this will prevent any leakage of media when you print.
- To use cover-film cut-outs for *negative* imagery, make a well on your screen, peel of the backing paper from the cover-film cut-outs and position them on the back of the screen. Getting the backing paper off can be fiddly and because of this, we normally use freezer paper or masking tape for negative images.

To print, pin or clamp down your prepared cloth. Use thickened dye paints, discharge paste or fabric paints. Work on dry cloth or wet-on-wet and process your cloth according to the media used.

Note: in addition to using cover film and freezer paper on the screen, you can apply both directly on to your cloth as a resist. Having done so, use a blank screen to apply your chosen media, or paint or scrape it on. This approach can be used for positive and negative imagery.

Tyvek has been taped to an aluminium plate and is now being cut with a fine soldering iron/hot pen; delicate imagery seems to work most effectively

Black cloth discharged with a Tyvek stencil

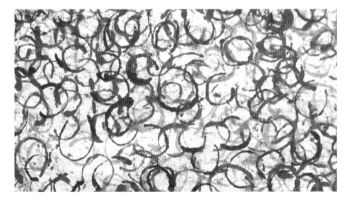

Cloth printed with dye paints and a Tyvek stencil

The same cloth as in the previous photograph, this time over-printed with an interfacing stencil before being over-dyed

Tyvek

Tyvek is a building material embraced by the embroidery community due to its ability to bubble and melt when heated with an air gun. It's also useful as a stencil material for fine line designs (not shapes) using a soldering iron or hot pen.

Depending on the design, Tyvek has the potential to be washed and re-used several times. You should be able to find it in any good building supply outlet.

- Place the screen on to a piece of Tyvek and draw around the perimeter. Cut this out of the sheet.
- Draw a line approximately 7cm/3" inside the outer perimeter: this provides a frame and will ensure your design doesn't go outside of the printable area of the screen.
- Place the Tyvek on to a piece of sheet metal or a glass plate, and anchor the four corners with masking tape.
- Heat up a soldering iron or 'hot pen' and carefully etch out fine lines. Be aware that designs that criss-cross or are long and curvy may bag and sag – we find that bridges are helpful when using Tyvek.
- Now trim the four edges of the stencil a little so it fits on to (but not right up to the edge of) the wooden frame of the screen.
- It can also be helpful to reinforce the edges of the stencil with Duck Tape before using it.

To use the Tyvek stencil, tape it to the back of the screen. If the design has 'floppy bits', spray the back of the stencil with 505/basting spray, then place the screen on top. The 505 will help the floppy bits stay put when you print. To print, pin or clamp down your prepared cloth. Use thickened dye paints, discharge paste or fabric paints. Work on dry cloth or wet-on-wet and process your cloth according to the media used.

Whilst Tyvek stencils won't last as long as fabric-based stencils, they can usually be washed, dried and re-used several times. To preserve them, let the screen sit in water for about 5 minutes; this softens up the masking tape and minimises the risk of tearing the stencil. When the masking tape has softened up, carefully peel it away, remove the Tyvek and rinse it gently. We often let the stencil soak in a pot of warm water before rinsing it out. Pat the stencil dry between an old towel and hang to dry thoroughly.

If you assisted the stencil with 505/basting spray, it may still feel tacky after washing, so store it between sheets of baking parchment.

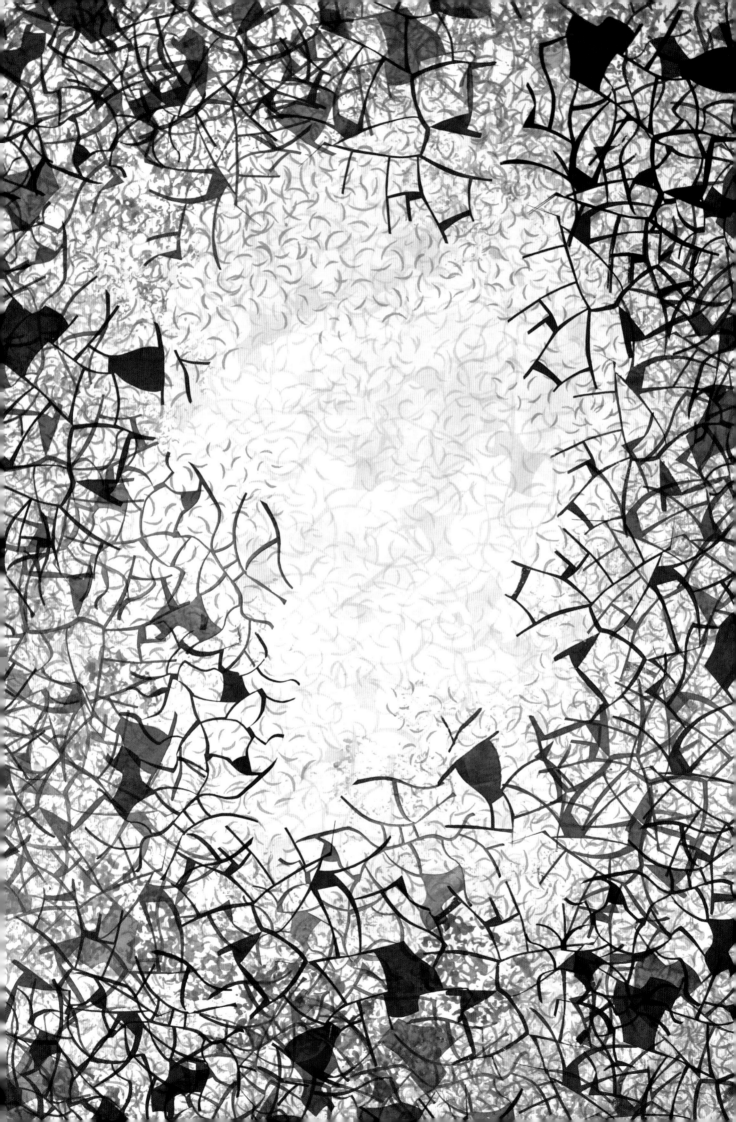

Fabric-based Stencils

Certain fabrics provide a great opportunity to make stencils with *positive or negative* imagery. Although they can take longer to make than other stencils, the time you initially invest is re-paid as they can be removed from the screen, washed and re-used many, many times.

One important point to remember is that these stencils will be taped to the back of the screen for printing. As such, any *negative imagery will print the shape of the screen*, resulting in squares and rectangles on your cloth. This can be fine, but sometimes you don't want squares and rectangles. To deal with this, we often paint the outer edges of these stencils to suit the imagery contained on them; sometimes simply 'feathering' the paint in from the edges, sometimes painting curved or jagged edges. How you tackle this depends on the imagery and the effect you're seeking. The photographs show examples - painting the outer edge also makes them firmer when you come to tape the stencil to the screen, and will make removal of the stencil easier.

Important Note: all of the following fabric-based stencils can stay on the screen indefinitely if used with thickened dye paints or discharge paste. Before re-using, start by placing the screen on an old towel, mist it with water and draw a squeegee across it a few times; this will clean it up and release any dried dye paint or discharge paste from the mesh. **DO NOT** leave stencils on the screen if you've used fabric paints – wash the screen and remove the stencil immediately. Otherwise, the paint can get trapped between the stencil and the mesh and set permanently.

Interfacing Stencils

Jane Dunnewold pioneered the use of interfacing as a stencil and Leslie went on to push the process further, adapting it and coming up with new variables.

Painted Interfacing Stencils

This approach enables you to create a re-useable stencil featuring *positive images, negatives images or both.* We've covered four different methods so do try as many as possible to find out what works best for you. Assemble the following materials - not necessarily all at once – you can start with simple approaches and move on to explore items such as Soy Wax resists when you're ready to.

For the basic approach, you'll need:
• lightweight, sew-in interfacing (such as Vilene or Pellon)
• a permanent marker pen (such as a laundry pen)
• a pot of cheap acrylic or water-based household paint in a pale colour
• a selection of mark-making tools such as brushes, needle-nose bottles, old credit cards, a piece of plastic for monoprinting etc.
• scissors
• a piece of sheet plastic.

To explore variables on the basic approach you'll need:
• freezer paper
• a small bottle of washable P.V.A. glue ('school glue')
• 1kg/2lbs of Soy Wax, something to melt it in and some dedicated (metal) tools to apply the wax
• spray acrylic paint in a pale colour
• webbing spray
• items to use a resists (construction mesh, net bags, old pieces of moulding, plastic doilies, bits of old lace etc.)

So, let's start with the basic approach of hand-painting.

Cloth printed with positive and negative imagery, and the stencils used to print it

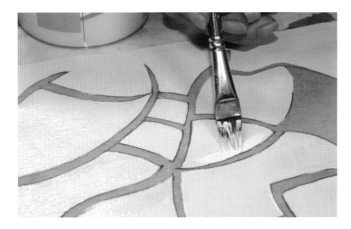
Painting around a drawn line to create positive imagery

Cloth printed with a positive image interfacing stencil

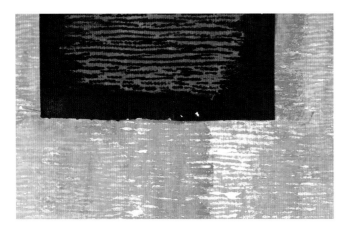
Printed cloth with its negative imagery stencil; the marks were created using a square-ended brush and acrylic paint, and the outer edges unevenly filled in

Hand-painting stencils:

- Lay out the interfacing and place the screen on top of it. Draw around the screen then cut using these guidelines. You'll trim the stencil later, but this is an easy way to start.
- In soft pencil, mark a frame about 7cm/3" inside the outer edges. This will ensure your design stays inside the printable area of the screen. To check this, lay the screen back on top of the stencil and make sure you can see the frame lines.
- If you have a specific design in mind, it can be helpful to trace or draw it on to the interfacing with a water-proof pen. If you're simply looking for texture or more spontaneous imagery, paint without tracing a design first.
- Place the interfacing on to a sheet of plastic and tape it down at the four edges with masking tape.
- Paint in the design or paint around the design: remember that the painted areas will act as a resist and the *open areas of interfacing will be what prints*, so:

    - filling in a drawn/traced design or painting inside it will generate a negative image
    - painting around/outside the drawn design/image will create a positive image

- The first layer of paint is the hardest to apply, as the interfacing tends to grab the brush. Go slowly and steadily in the knowledge that the second (and possibly third) coats will be easier.
- Leave the stencil on it's plastic to dry as it will make the next layer easier: you'll probably need to paint in the design about three times as the paint needs to completely fill the interfacing to resist well. To check that it's fully sealed, hold the painted interfacing up to the light. If you can see light coming through it, media will be able to come through it, so keep re-painting or plan to leave the interfacing incompletely sealed; this approach gives a textural quality when you come to print.
- *Note;* if you've worked in the negative, consider giving the edges of the stencil an appropriate 'treatment' in paint to avoid printing squares or rectangles. We like to feather in the edges to give a soft edge to the print, or mimic the angles of the painted design (take a look at the pictures and you'll see what we mean).
- When the stencil is ready:

    - trim it slightly to it sits nicely on the wooden frame of the screen; you want to see about 1 1/2cm/1/2" of wood as this gives you a nice edge to tape the stencil to the screen.
    - place it in between two layers of parchment paper and iron it with a dry iron set to cotton. This will fix the paint to the interfacing.

There are many, many variables to the basic hand-painting approach. Just remember, the areas where you applied acrylic/household paint will act as a resist, so it's the spaces you leave open and free from paint that will generate the design once you come to print with the stencil. Other ways forward with hand painting include:

• Use a square, blunt-ended brush to apply layers of texture (see the photograph at the bottom of the previous page).
• Paint out negative shapes in order to generate positive line imagery, or vice versa.
• Use something other than a paintbrush to apply the paint; a roller will create textural effects, old credit cards for stamping lines or scraping the paint on, monoprinting, doodling, writing or sketching with a needle-nose bottle. If you have them, use thermofax screens or screens with permanent designs on them to print the paint on; you'll generate a reverse image on the stencil.

Note how we've feathered the edges of this negative image texture stencil to avoid printing a hard edge rectangle

Whatever approach you take, acknowledge that you'll need apply about three layers of paint. Lining up marks or prints two or three times is difficult but don't get anxious about it - accept that you'll get an organic look. Remember to wash out your tools in between layers of paint application.

We know that some people find hand painting difficult or tedious. Here are some alternative approaches to creating positive and negative designs. They still require work (nothing in life is free) but will give you some interesting variables to play with.

**Work-in-progress
by Allie Heath**

Painting on top of freezer paper resists

Ironing freezer paper on to interfacing before you paint it will create a temporary resist. After you've applied the paint the paper is removed and the design will be revealed as the open, printable part of the stencil:

- Positive images: to generate a positive image on the stencil, iron on shapes or lines that have been cut or torn out of freezer paper. You may have to iron on the elements of the design one by one.
- Negative images: if you want a negative image stencil, cut imagery into the freezer paper, and iron on the piece that's had the design cut from it.

1. *Position your freezer paper on to the interfacing. This photograph shows cut shapes which will act as a resist and generate a positive image stencil. Iron the freezer paper into position using parchment to protect the interfacing.*

3. *Alternatively, apply several thin layers of paint using a blank screen as this tends to minimise the paint creeping under the freezer paper resist. If you do use a screen, wash it up immediately after use.*

4. *When the final coat of paint is dry, peel off the freezer paper, trim the stencil slightly and touch up or feather in the edges if you've worked in the negative image.*

Note; avoid using masking tape or cover film as resists, as we find they can tear the interfacing when taken off.

2. *Now apply several <u>thin</u> layers of paint allowing each coat to dry fully before applying the next one. These layers of paint can be applied using a brush, but work carefully and avoid pushing paint under the edges of the freezer paper resist.*

Washable P.V.A. Glue

Using washable P.V.A. glue as a resist on the interfacing before you apply paint will generate positive imagery:

1. Place the interfacing on plastic and tape it down at the four edges.
2. Use Washable P.V.A. glue to apply the design, making sure it fully penetrates the interfacing. Leave to dry flat on the plastic.
3. When the resist is completely dry (leave it overnight if possible), use a blank screen or brush to apply several thin layers of acrylic/household paint over the stencil with its P.V.A. design. Again, you may need to apply up to 3 layers, leaving the stencil in place and washing out your tools in between applications.

5. Pat the stencil dry in a folded towel and hang to dry. If it buckles slightly, iron it flat under parchment before use.
6. Trim the edges if necessary.

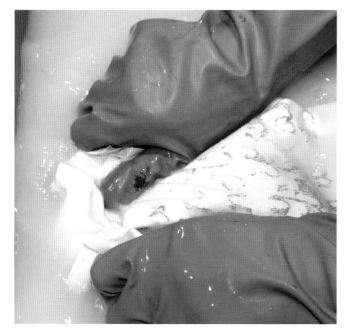

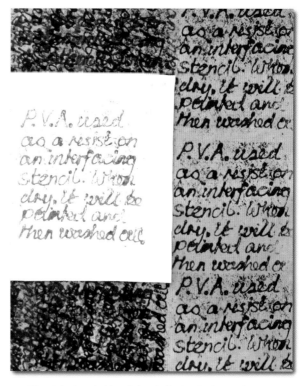

4. When the final layer of paint is completely dry (ideally, leave it overnight), trim the stencil slightly and then soak it in hot water for 10 minutes, then gently rub away the resist. Don't scrub aggressively or you can tear the exposed interfacing. Some traces of painted P.V.A. may stay put, but we find this adds to – rather than detracts from – the effect.

The right hand side of the cloth clearly shows the text created by writing with P.V.A. The left hand side shows how texture is created by multiple layers of printing

Stamping hot soy wax on to interfacing with a cookie cutter

Soy wax was used as the resist for this painted interfacing stencil. It was used on cloth that had been previously printed with a Tyvek stencil. Finally, the cloth was over-dyed

A selection of painted stencils using soy wax as the resist

Painting on top of soy wax resist

Soy wax is a very good alternative to Batik wax. It's non-toxic, biodegradable and can be removed from cloth with hot water. If you decide to invest in it, do not melt it in a wax pot that's had Batik wax in it. If soy wax is mixed with bee or paraffin wax, it will wash out but the others won't. Invest in a new pot and new tools. Whilst we're using it as a resist on a stencil, it can also be used directly on cloth in the usual manner of Batik and have dye paints applied over it. Later on in the book, we'll also cover how to use it as a resist on the screen itself. To use it as a resist to generate positive imagery on painted stencils, follow this procedure:

- Use masking tape to secure the interfacing to a piece of plastic.
- Apply the soy wax, working in a manner that ensures it penetrates the interfacing. You can use:

  - Tjantings; Indonesian Batik 'pens' that allow you to draw, write or doodle. They take a bit of practise to use, but are worth it. Let the bowl end sit in the hot wax before using them.
  - Tjaps: Indonesian copper stamps – let them heat up in the hot wax, lift out, tamp off the excess on paper towel and stamp wax on to the interfacing.
  - Metal scrapers: wallpaper scrapers are great for line imagery. Let the ends heat up in the hot wax, then stamp with them.
  - Bristle brushes: again, let the bristles heat up in the hot wax, then paint the wax on. This approach will generate more fragile marks in areas where the wax hasn't fully penetrated the interfacing, but this can make great effects.
  - Found objects: anything metal will work well as it will keep the wax hot and fluid. Experiment with flat-headed nails hammered into a block of wood, metal pill packets glued to wood blocks, cookie cutters etc.

- When the wax is dry (which only takes a minute), use a blank screen or brush to apply several thin layers of acrylic/household paint over the stencil. Again, you may need to apply up to 3 layers, letting each layer dry completely and leaving the stencil in place on the plastic.
- Wash out your tools in between applications of paint.
- When the final layer of paint is completely dry (and we'd recommend leaving it overnight), trim the stencil slightly and then soak it in hot water for 10 minutes, and then gently rub away the soy wax. Even though it has paint over it, the wax will wash away. Some traces of paint may have leached through the wax but again, we find this adds to the overall effect (and don't scrub aggressively or you can tear the exposed interfacing).
- Pat the stencil dry in a folded towel and hang to dry. If it buckles slightly, iron it flat under parchment before use.

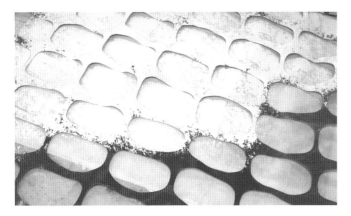
Construction mesh laid over interfacing and stencilled

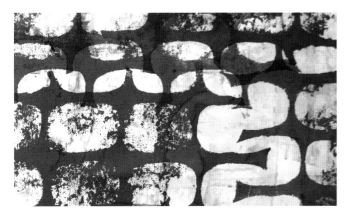
Cloth printed with the construction mesh interfacing stencil

Spraying interfacing with webbing spray

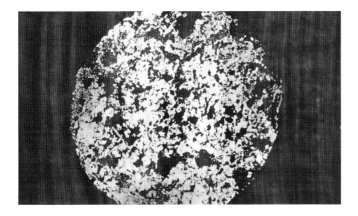
Dye painted cloth, dishcharged using a webbing spray interfacing stencil

Stencilling & spray painting:

Another way to apply paint is by stencilling or spraying. If you decide to explore this you'll need:

- A can of spray acrylic in a pale colour
- Items to use as a resist
- An old cardboard box to use as a spray booth, or work outside on a still day.

We've explored lots of found objects to use as resists including construction mesh, net vegetable bags, sink liners, decorative plastic moulding, plastic doilies, old lace and so forth. Whatever you use, let's assume your interfacing is cut to the size you want it, you've drawn a frame to work within and taped it at the four corners to a piece of sheet plastic. Now…

- Place the item you're using as a resist on to the interfacing, within the drawn frame.
- If the resist isn't suitable for use with a stencil brush, spray on lots of thin layers of acrylic paint making sure you direct the spray from above, rather than the side. This will minimise paint blowing under a resist such as construction mesh. Let each layer of paint dry fully before applying the next one, and work outside on a still day or use an old cardboard box as a spray booth.
- If the resist item you're using is suitable for stencilling, you can apply acrylic or household paint using a stiff stencil brush. Remember to apply several thin layers of paint rather than trying to seal the interfacing in one go.
- Whether you spray paint or stencil from time to time, carefully pick up the plastic – along with the interfacing and resist - to check if the interfacing is fully sealed with paint. Remember, if you can see light coming through the paint, media will come through when you come to print with the stencil.
- When you're satisfied, remove the item you used as a resist, trim the stencil and heat-set it between two layers of parchment.

Webbing spray:

Another approach to spray-painting that achieves a beautiful, textural effect is to spray with webbing spray (found in most craft/art or hobby outlets). It's similar to 'silly string' and sprays in a random, erratic manner laying down wiggly lines of paint. It will create a negative image for you (e.g. the gaps in between the webbing spray will be what prints). Do try to find it as it's very effective. To use it:

- Spread out a few sheets of newspaper and practise with the webbing spray: spray from close-up or from a distance. Move your hand quickly or slowly, up and down or from side to side.
- When you know what you like, tape a piece of interfacing to some plastic and lay it on fresh newspaper.
- Use your preferred technique to spray on the webbing spray; several layers will create a closer textural effect whilst one or two layers will create a more open textural effect.
- When you're finished, let the sprayed stencil dry out completely, then trim it before use.

So, you've now got a painted interfacing stencil (or several). How do you use it...

1. *Choose a screen appropriate to the size of the stencil and create a well on the back.*

4. *To print, pin or clamp down your prepared cloth, which can be white or pre-coloured. If pre-coloured, acknowledge that it will affect any subsequent colours you put on it. Work on dry cloth or wet-on-wet for bleed effects.*

2. *Place the stencil on the back of the screen and using a double layer of torn or straight-edge masking tape, secure it to the screen. Remember the stencil can be used either way up so be aware you have the ability to reverse the design.*

3. *You can now print with thickened dye paints, discharge paste or fabric paints. If you use fabric paints, be sure to keep the screen wet and in use otherwise the fabric paint can have a tendency to clog and block the stencil.*

5. *Make your first print on a drop cloth or a piece of junk fabric. To begin with, the open areas of interfacing will soak up the media and you may have to add more. Once you get a good print, move to your prepared cloth.*

One important aspect to note is that the interfacing will hold on to the media it has soaked up. With coloured media, such as thickened dye paint or fabric paint, if you add a new colour, the residue colour left in the interfacing will contaminate it. This is something to exploit, rather than get frustrated about, for example:

- Jane Dunnewold teaches a method using thickened dye paint or fabric paints. Starting with yellow, you then move to orange, then red, then purple and then blue – printing the rainbow spectrum on cloth. Or, you could start with yellow, then add green, then blue, then purple and finish with red.
- Leslie likes to work in variations of the same colour. For example, you could work back and forth with scarlet and magenta and then add a touch (or more!) of red-brown or brown. Or, you could mix thickened dye paint in every colour of blue you have, and print with these.
- Once the stencil is saturated with colour, you can change the value by using print paste, and then go back to using colour. If using fabric paints, use transparent extender base to create paler values.
- Streaky effects are possible by adding a bead of the main colour, then placing a dot of a second colour on top of it; when you print, the second colour will cause a streak.

- As you print, you'll lay down your imagery but also leave white areas (unless you're printing on coloured cloth). Experiment with over-printing to really develop layers of colour, value, texture and imagery.
- When finished, drop the screen - with its stencil still attached - into a sink or tray of warm water. Let it soak for 5 minutes or so. Soaking softens the masking tape and makes it easier to remove the stencil.
- Carefully peel off the masking tape and remove the stencil from the screen.
- Wash it carefully in warm water; support it with your hands or use a litter tray. When wet and off the screen, the stencil is at its most fragile and could rip. Consider soaking it in a pot of warm water.
- When clean, either dry with a towel, or hang and drip dry.
- If the stencil buckles on drying, place it between two layers of parchment and iron it to flatten it out.
- If looked after, this type of stencil will last years.

Process your printed cloth according to the media used.

The interfacing has been saturated with paint and dried. It's now being cut with a screw punch

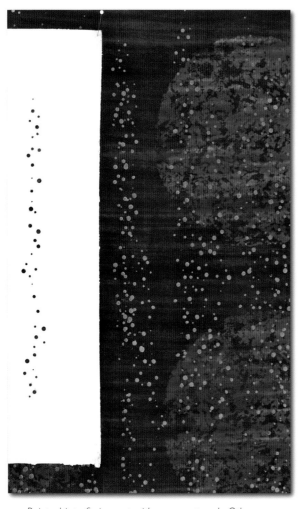

Painted interfacing, cut with a screw punch. Other designs can be achieved by cutting with a craft knife

PAINTED & CUT INTERFACING STENCILS

This approach involves sealing a piece of interfacing with several coats of water-based paint, resulting in a flexible, waterproof stencil material that will allow you to cut out positive images. The imagery you'll be creating can be as intricate as you like. Assemble the following materials:

- Lightweight, sew-in interfacing (such as Vilene or Pellon)
- A can of cheap acrylic or water-based household paint. Avoid black - choose a pale colour.
- Scissors
- A piece of sheet plastic
- Craft knife & cutting mat (or an old lino tile will do)
- A can of temporary basting spray (such as 505), although you won't need this until you use the stencil on the screen.

Making the Stencil

- Cut out a piece of interfacing by drawing around the screen (you'll trim it down later).
- Mark a frame about 7cm/2" inside the outer edges.
- At this stage, you have the option of drawing or tracing your design on to the interfacing using a waterproof pen such as a 'Sharpie' or a pencil. Designs can be as complex and intricate as you like, but acknowledge you'll be cutting them out with a craft knife, so patience will be required.
- Tape the interfacing down on to a piece of plastic at the four corners.
- Using a roller or household paintbrush, paint the entire surface with acrylic or household paint. Leave the painted stencil on the plastic and either hang it up to dry, or leave to dry flat. If you can hang it in sunlight, it'll dry quite quickly, otherwise, this first layer of paint could take overnight to dry.
- Now apply another coat of paint; you may need to do this a third or even fourth time as the aim is to completely seal the interfacing. It can stay on the plastic sheet as you do this. Allow each layer of paint to dry out completely before adding additional coats.
- To check that it's fully sealed, peel the stencil off the plastic and hold it up to the light: if you can see light coming through it, media will be able to come through it, so keep re-painting or...
- Allow it to be incompletely sealed; this approach allows for extra texture when you come to print.
- Now place the painted interfacing in between two layers of parchment paper and iron it with a dry iron set to cotton. This will fix the paint to the interfacing.
- Place it on to a cutting mat and use masking tape to secure at the four corners.
- Cut out the design using a craft knife. If you pre-drew a design, it should still be visible through several layers of paint. Remember that what you cut is what you'll print and any design will work – even shapes that may sag and bag.
- *Optional:* it's possible to use a soldering iron or hot pen to 'cut' out a design. It gives a ragged, more organic edge. If you choose this option, work in a well ventilated area as there'll be some fumes. We find that the best results are achieved if the stencil is taped to a piece of glass or aluminium sheet. Get the soldering iron good and hot, then use it as a pen to burn out the design.

Don't be afraid to cut out complex designs... even ones with 'flappy bits'. The black squares are pieces of iron-on interfacing used to repair tears

Place the stencil on newspaper and spray it with a re-positionable glue such as 505

Move the sprayed stencil to the drop cloth, carefully position the screen before placing it on the stencil

Secure the edges with two layers of masking tape to prevent bleed; the repositionable glue will ensure the floppy edges of the design stay put during printing

Attaching the stencil to the screen

If your cut stencil has no floppy or baggy bits, simply tape it to the back of the screen using two layers of masking tape as described on page 38. However, if it does have floppy bits, you may be looking at it and thinking; "how am I going to get these to stay flat when I'm printing?". Don't worry, a student of ours (Elaine Griffiths), came up with the perfect solution:

• Place the stencil on a piece of newspaper, reverse side up (the side that will be attached to the back of the screen should face up). These stencils are reversible, so the choice is yours.
• Spray the back of the stencil with a fine layer of 505/basting spray, then lift it off the newspaper (which is thrown away) and place it on a drop cloth.
• Carefully position the screen over the stencil, hovering and checking that the design is well positioned. Lower the screen on to the stencil and use a squeegee to press the mesh down.
• Flip the screen over; the stencil is now temporarily attached to the mesh with the basting spray.
• Seal the edges of the stencil with two layers of masking tape to prevent leakage of media.

Use & cleaning:

• To print, pin or clamp down your prepared cloth. Use thickened dye paints, discharge paste or fabric paints. Work on dry cloth or wet-on-wet.
• When finished, drop the screen - with its stencil still attached - into a sink or box of cold/warm water. Let it soak for 5 minutes or so. Soaking softens the masking tape and makes it easier to remove the stencil.
• Carefully peel off the masking tape borders.
• Peel off the stencil and wash it carefully in warm water; support it with your hands or use a litter tray. When wet and off the screen the stencil is at its most fragile and could rip. We often let the stencil soak in a pot of warm water before rinsing it thoroughly.
• When clean, pat it dry between a towel, or hang and drip dry
• If you assisted the stencil with 505/basting spray, it may still feel tacky after washing, so store it between sheets of baking parchment.
• If the stencil buckles on drying, place it between two layers of parchment and iron it to flatten it out. If looked after, this type of stencil will last years.

Process your printed cloth according to the media used.

You'll need 3 to 6 layers of web, although we find it easier to bond them to the interfacing one at a time

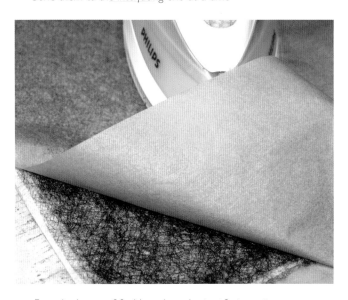

Fuse the layers of fusible web to the interfacing, using parchment to protect the iron

Once the fusible web is adhered to the interfacing, feather in the edges to give a softer-edged print and make the edges more robust

INTERFACING & FUSIBLE WEB

Interfacing combined with layers of fusible web makes a fabulous, textural stencil. You will need:

- Lightweight, sew-in interfacing (such as Vilene or Pellon)
- Fusible web (such as Misty Fuse or Fuse FX)
- Parchment paper
- An iron
- Acrylic or household paint
- A brush

To make the stencil:

- Cut out a piece of interfacing and up to 6 pieces of fusible web by drawing around the screen the stencil is to be used with.
- The number of layers of web will determine the textural quality of the print. We find that at least three layers are needed, and more will generate a more fragile looking print.
- Lay down a piece of parchment paper, slightly larger than the cut interfacing and web pieces.
- Place the interfacing on top of the parchment and place the first piece of fusible web on top of that. Cover with a second layer of parchment.
- Fuse the web to the interfacing using a dry iron set to wool. Work slowly and steadily to make sure you get a good bond.
- Peel away the top layer of parchment paper, add the second layer of web, replace the top layer of parchment and fuse.
- Repeat this process with as many layers of fusible web as you wish – remember that the more layers you use, the more fragile the resulting print.
- Finally, trim the stencil edges by about 1cm/^''' and consider feathering them in with acrylic/household paint to give a softer, organic print – this will also make the edges more robust.

Using a fusible web stencil is similar to using a painted stencil, so rather than repeat ourselves, read the notes on pages 38 to 39.

Cloth being printed with a fusible web stencil. Two colours of thickened dye are being used to create a lovely background texture

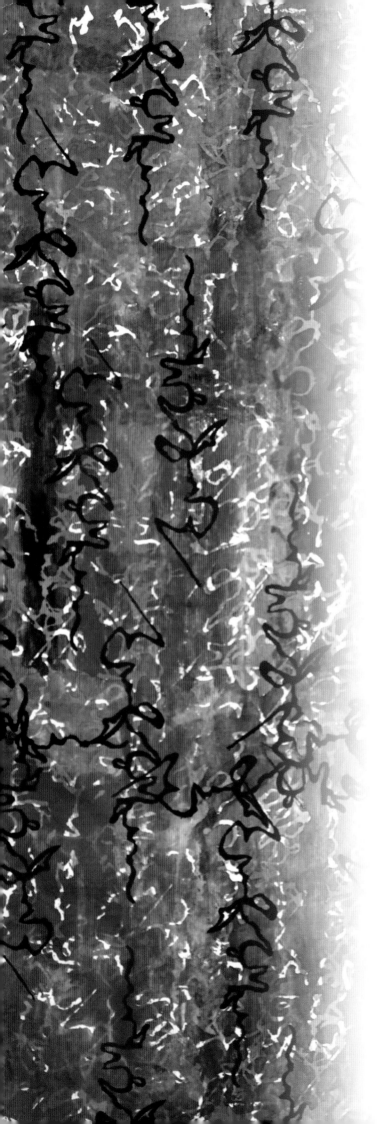

PAPER LAMINATION STENCILS

'Paper & Metal Leaf Lamination; a mixed media approach with cloth' is a book of ours co-authored with Jane Dunnewold. It explores the lamination process in great depth but we wanted to include one aspect in this book, as it's a great way of making stencils. They can be taped to the back of a silkscreen, or pinned down on top of cloth. You will need:

- Newspaper or photocopy paper
- Polyester curtain sheer (a half metre will be fine to begin with)
- A screen, with some kind of design on it (so you could use any of the approaches covered in this book!). Or you can use a brush, a needle-nose bottle, a stencil or a scraper.
- Fluid Matte Medium; a clear, fluid acrylic binder - Golden & Liquitex are very good brands.
- A small pot of acrylic paint in any colour.
- Pins.
- An iron.
- Parchment paper.

Now work through the following steps:

Assemble and arrange the paper(s):

1. Work on a print table covered with a drop cloth.
2. Cut a piece of polyester voile/organza about 2cm/1" larger than the screen you plan to use it with.
3. Lay out newspaper or photocopy paper with the edges slightly over-lapping; create an area that's slightly smaller than the size of the piece of voile you're using.

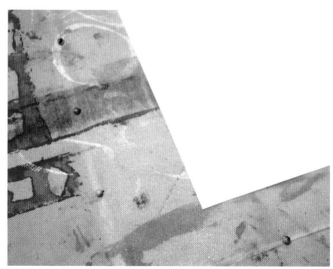

Cover the laid-out paper with sheer fabric and pin down:

4. Gently float the voile down over the collaged papers.
5. Pin the cloth down carefully – about every 5cm/2" – and place it under some tension as you pin. Pinning through paper can be difficult, which is why we suggest that the paper collage is slightly smaller than the voile. Good pinning takes time but is important as when you print the matte medium, the sheer cloth will try to follow the wet screen when you pick it up. You want the sheer to stay in contact with the papers and pinning will encourage it to stay put.

Apply the matte medium:

6. Matte Medium is used to 'laminate' or bond the paper permanently to the cloth. Whilst it looks white in the bottle, it dries clear. When making stencils, we like to add a drop of acrylic paint to the matte medium to tint it slightly. This makes it easier to see where you've applied it. It can be applied it to the fabric surface in one of several ways:

- If you're printing with a thermofax or a silk-screen, pour (tinted) matte medium out at the edge of the screen and use the squeegee to pull it across the surface. Use plenty of pressure and make enough passes (one to three, depending on the design of the screen) to push the medium firmly on to the fabric, penetrating the cloth and adhering to the paper underneath.
- If you're painting with a brush, fill the brush with (tinted) matte medium and make several strokes across the surface. Use pressure as you stroke to make sure the matte medium penetrates the fabric and adheres to the paper underneath.
- If you're stencilling use a good, natural bristle stencil brush and apply the (tinted) matte medium in an even layer. Pounce with pressure, so the medium penetrates the fabric and adheres to the paper underneath.
- If you have the patience, draw or doodle with a needle-nose bottle. Acknowledge the lines will spread somewhat as the medium settles, so allow for this.

Whilst you don't want to splosh the Matte Medium on, you need to use enough to penetrate the sheer and saturate the paper. *Remember; the paper will only laminate to the cloth where you apply the (tinted) matte medium.* Once the matte medium has been applied, leave the piece on the bench for about 10 minutes then hang it up and allow it to dry completely.

Wash up your tools:

7. Wash your tools out the minute you've finished with them as otherwise, the matte medium may seal the mesh and bond permanently on the tool.

Heat set the dried laminated piece:

8. The laminated fabric will take from 30 minutes to dry (if hung in direct sunlight) to several hours or even overnight (if the atmosphere is damp or humid). Once the piece is dry, place it on the padded workbench and iron it with a dry iron (set to cotton) under baking parchment. Don't be lazy with heat-setting.

Soak the dried and heat-set piece:

9. Once the piece is dry and heat setting is complete, transfer the fabric/paper layer to a bucket or sink of cold or lukewarm water. The water should NOT be hot. Submerge the paper/fabric combination and soak it for five to ten minutes. During this time the paper will begin to soften, which makes it easier to remove.
10. Spread out plastic sheeting on the worktable to protect it. When the soaking time has elapsed, squeeze out the excess water and transfer the whole thing to the protected print bench or separate table. Lay it out flat, with the paper side up.

Using a painted interfacing stencil to print on the tinted matte medium

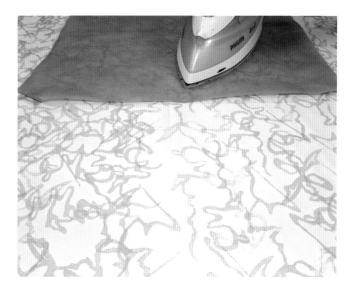

When the matte medium is completely dry, heat set the layer under parchment

Now soak the laminated cloth in a bucket of warm (but not hot) water; you'll see the un-laminated paper peel away

To start with, use your hands to scrub away the excess paper

You can gently scrub the surface with a pan scourer to get rid of more paper

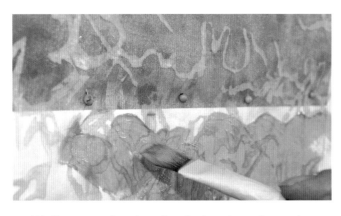

We like to treat the edges of our laminated stencils to make them stronger and avoid printing a hard-edged rectangle

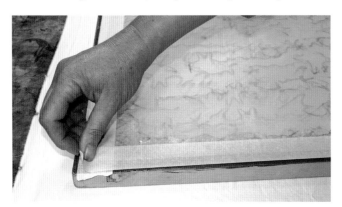

Create a well on the back of the screen before securing the stencil with more masking tape

Scrub off the excess paper:

11. Use your hands, a sponge or a washcloth to scrub away the paper attached to the cloth. The paper may peel off in layers at first, which is fine. Dump the waste in a litter tray or bucket as you progress, NOT down the sink. Where the matte medium has been applied, the paper will 'split' – imagine the paper being comprised of two very fine layers. The back will peel off quite easily, leaving the front layer behind. Don't worry about getting every scrap of paper off, jut make sure you get rid of all the un-laminated paper.
12. Shake the piece out, rinse it by hand, hose it down or run it through the rinse cycle of your washing machine (cold water) to get rid of any paper/pulp residue, and hang the fabric to dry.
13. Iron the laminated fabric under parchment to smooth any wrinkles that don't fall out as the fabric dries.
14. If you wish to, consider treating the edges of the stencil to generate a softer-edged print (it will otherwise print the shape of your screen; a square or rectangle). There are two ways to do this.

• Paint the edges with acrylic, using the design as a guide. You'll need to do this many times to seal the voile completely. Heat-set the stencil under parchment to set the paint. Or...
• Assemble 4 strips of paper that are a suitable width to create a border to the stencil.
• Lay one strip down and position one edge of the stencil on top of it. Pin both down.
• Now lay down the second strip, sliding it under the laminated stencil and pin down. Repeat until the stencil is edged with four underlying strips of paper. Paint over the strips in a manner suitable to the stencil design using (tinted) matte medium. Let everything dry, heat set under parchment and then soak and scrub off the excess paper. This is a quicker way of edging your stencil and will make it more robust. (Take a look at the photograph on the left and you'll get the idea).

Use & cleaning

Having made the laminated stencil, trim it slightly to fit the screen. To use it, simply tape it to the back of the screen. It can be used either way up so remember you have the ability to reverse the design.

Here we're using several colours of dye paint in the screen at once

The resulting print

Nearly finished

- You can print with thickened dye paints, discharge paste or fabric paints.
- To print, pin or clamp down your prepared cloth, which can be white or pre-coloured. If pre-coloured, acknowledge that it will affect any subsequent colours you put on it.
- If using discharge paste, always test a small patch first to make sure the cloth will discharge.
- Work on dry, damp or wet cloth.
- When finished, drop the screen - with its stencil still attached - into a sink or tray of warm water. Let it soak for 5 minutes or so. Soaking softens the masking tape and makes it easier to remove the stencil.
- Carefully remove the masking tape, peel off the stencil and wash it carefully in warm water.
- When clean, dry with a towel or hang to drip dry.
- If the stencil buckles on drying, place it between two layers of parchment and iron it.
- If looked after, this type of stencil will last years.
- Process your printed cloth according to the media used.

Once you've got the hang of this process you can make stencils any size you like. Super-size ones can be pinned over cloth and have media scraped through them, or you can use a blank screen to push media through them.

Paper Lamination is a fascinating process in itself, so if you feel you'd like to take it further, then seek out our book, '**Paper & Metal Leaf Lamination; a mixed media approach with cloth**'.

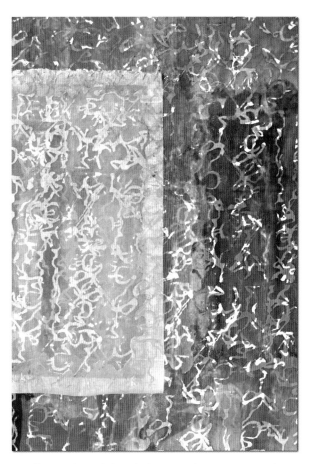

The resulting cloth with the paper lamination stencil used to print it

Semi-permanent Designs

The following two approaches enable you to create designs on the screen that will last a long time, but which are removable when you're done with them. Because of their longevity, we've chosen to cover them separately rather than including them in the 'Temporary Resist' section.

SOY WAX

We've already spoken about soy wax on page 36, but let's recap. It's a great alternative to traditional Batik wax – generally a mixture of beeswax and paraffin wax. It can be washed out from screens, tools or your cloth with hot water (60°F). Being non-toxic and biodegradable, it won't clog up your pipes or harm the environment. We use a crockpot/slow cooker and a traditional wax pot for melting the soy wax in.

Whilst it was designed as a substitute for Batik wax for direct applications on to cloth, it's a perfect candidate for creating temporary but long-lasting designs on the screen, which will print in the *negative* image.

Reminder: do not mix soya wax and bee or paraffin wax together. If you're going to use a wax pot that's previously had bee or paraffin wax in it, you must get rid of this completely. If not, you'll be back to ironing out the wax and dry-cleaning/boiling the cloth.

Assemble the following:

- Soy wax (about 1 kg/2lbs)
- A dedicated pot for melting the wax in
- Tools; tjantings, bristle brushes etc
- A dry, clean screen
- Several sheets of newspaper
- A roll of kitchen paper/paper towel

Follow these guidelines:

- Make sure the wax is fully melted and hot to ensure good results. Soy wax is very versatile as it cools more slowly than other wax types but still dries quickly.
- Apply the wax to the back of the screen; try brushes (bristle or foam), tjaps (Indonesian copper stamps), tjanting (Indonesian metal wax 'pens'), metal scrapers, cookie cutters, through a stencil etc. We find it's helpful to tamp off excess wax from the tool on to a folded piece of paper towel. Remember, the wax is the resist and therefore the design will be printed in the negative image when you come to use the screen.
- Let the wax dry (which won't take long). As soon as it's dry, your screen is ready to use.
- Pin or clamp out cloth that's been prepared accordingly for the media you're going to use to print the screen; thickened dye paint, discharge paste or fabric paint will all work well.
- Print with your chosen media. You should find that the wax resist will last a long time; we have one screen that's been in use for 6 months.
- Wash the screen in cold water to clean it (not hot).

- Process and rinse the cloth according to the media you've used (see pages 61 to 69 for guidance).
- When you're ready to reclaim the screen, simply scrub it with a brush in hot water to remove the soy wax; it will wash out at 60°F or hotter, but will not be removable with cold water.
- If particles of soy wax get deposited on your cloth during the printing process, don't panic. Process or cure the cloth according to the media used, then simply wash it at 60°F; the wax will wash away.

Crock pot, wax pot and various tools used with Soy Wax

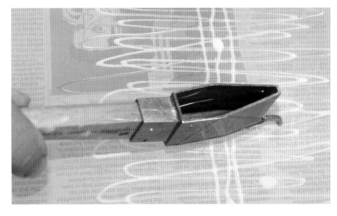

Drawing soy wax on to the back of the screen using a tjanting

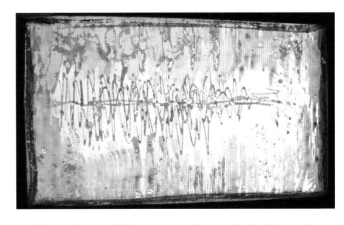

Having drawn with the tjanting, we then used a brush to apply wax around the edges of the screen

DRAWING FLUID & SCREEN FILLER

Screen filler creates a long-lasting, semi-permanent image on the screen. It should be removed from the screen within 3 months of application and may wear away before that, but you'll get hundreds and hundreds of prints before this happens. The filler is applied by pulling it over the whole screen with a squeegee. In addition to the guidelines we've provided here, please read the manufacturers' instructions.

Assemble the following:

• A blank, clean and dry screen
• 'Speedball' Drawing Fluid and Screen Filler
• A selection of tools; try paint brushes (foam and bristle), and needle-nose bottles to begin with.
• A piece of acrylic sheet if you wish to monoprint
• Several sheets of newspaper
• A cat litter tray for resting the screen on

Imagery can be achieved by either applying Drawing Fluid onto the screen first, or by direct application of filler. Let's take a look at both approaches.

Applying a design with Drawing Fluid

Drawing Fluid is a water-based resist which when dry, prevents the Screen Filler from filling the mesh in the imaged area, creating a positive image. When the fluid is dry, filler is pulled across the screen and also left to dry. The screen is then washed to remove the drawing fluid. For precision images/designs;

3. *Flip the screen over and using your drawn lines as a guide, paint the Drawing Fluid on to the back of the screen. Fine lines may be obliterated by the filler 'relaxing' into the spaces so when painting on the drawing fluid, make fine lines between 10-25% larger than you want them. You can narrow lines that are too wide by touching up with screen filler later.*

1. *Trace or draw your design onto the inner (front) surface of your screen with a soft pencil. Drawing on the inner/front surface is important as the mesh will be flat on the table and you won't accidentally pierce it with the pencil, and lettering will be the correct way around.*
2. *Remember that you're working in the positive image; what you draw is what you'll ultimately print.*

For free designs;

4. *Achieve interesting textures or patterns by applying drawing fluid 'freestyle'. Just stamp, dribble, doodle or brush it on to the mesh. Try printing with leaves, fan brushes, corks etc. Try using a needle-nose bottle to doodle, dribble, write or draw. Again, remember that the drawing fluid design will eventually print the positive image.*
5. *If you apply the fluid to plastic and then 'etch' into it, you can then take a mono print by placing the screen down on top of the design (lay the screen flat to dry when you're done).*
6. *You can stand the screen upright and let drawing fluid dribble down it.*

Let the applied drawing fluid dry completely (sometimes overnight). Check you've applied enough to create a good resist by holding the screen up to the light once it's dry. The imaged areas should be a solid blue and not too pale, although they'll be shiny and slightly tacky to the touch. Remember that fine lines can be obliterated by the thickness of the screen filler rolling over them, so add more width to the design - make them 10-25% larger than you want them.

For a truly tight resist it can be worth applying a second coat of drawing fluid to the inner/front side of the screen, although this isn't possible with some application processes such as monoprinting! If you do apply a second layer, let the first layer of drawing fluid dry out completely then flip the screen over, support it on two battens or a cat litter tray to raise it clear of the table and re-paint it from the other side.

Note; you can also use Soy Wax as an alternative to Drawing Fluid. It has the advantage of setting almost immediately but ultimately, the quality of mark you're seeking will determine your choice.

Applying the Screen Filler

In our experience, people get scared when applying the filler. Be bold, have a go and acknowledge you can touch up/fill in any thin areas later.

1. *Shake the tub of screen filler in advance to ensure that the filler is well-mixed, but air bubbles have had time to pop.*
2. *Cover a surface with newspaper or work on a washable surface; this stage is messy and you'll be working fast.*
3. *Place the screen mesh (back) side up on a flat surface.*
4. *You're looking to fill the screen mesh with a coating of filler that's thick enough to create a semi-permanent resist, but not so thick that excess drips through, causing lumps and bumps on the front of the mesh/screen.*

6. *Keep going right off the edge of the screen, drawing off the excess filler on to the newspaper. You can scoop it up with a spatula and put it back in the tub later.*
7. *If you get uneven coverage, don't panic. It's best to let the filler dry and touch up any thin parts with a brush later.*
8. *Let the screen dry horizontally and if the frame edges are really messy, carefully wipe them down. Ideally, let the screen sit overnight to ensure the filler dries out completely.*

The linear marks on this piece of cloth were created with a drawing fluid and screen filler design. We used the screen with discharge paste and over-printed the cloth later with fabric paint

5. *A such, pour a generous bead of screen filler edge-to-edge across the right/top side of the screen (judging the amount becomes easier with practise). The minute you've placed your bead, the filler will start running through the mesh, so pull the squeegee immediately across the screen, moving firmly and steadily and keeping the squeegee close to upright.*

Cloth printed with a screen filler semi-permanent screen

Washing out the drawing fluid

Once the screen filler is completely dry, you can wash out the drawing fluid:

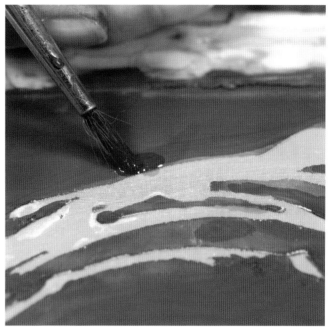

1. *Start by using cold water and gently rubbing the areas filled with drawing fluid with a sponge. If the fluid is resistant, use warm water and a scourer or brush. If part of the drawing fluid design has been coated with filler, scrub it until it comes away.*
2. *When the drawing fluid has been washed/scrubbed out, you'll have clear areas of mesh that will print in the positive image.*
3. *Let the screen dry before use, or before touching up.*

5. *Over time and through use, the filler may erode and you may need to repair/touch up areas of the design.*
6. *Touching up - making lines thinner, filling small gaps or areas of poor coverage, re-filling worn out areas etc. - can be done by painting in more filler.*
7. *Let any new filler dry out completely before using the screen.*

Touching Up/Repairs

4. *To check the coverage of the filler, hold the screen up to the light and make sure all of the filled areas are totally opaque. Look out for pinholes from bubbles in the filler, areas of poor coverage or accidental damage caused by vigorous removal of the drawing fluid. Consider your lines to check they're the thickness you want them.*

• *Note: if you decide you adore the screen and want it forever, consider making repairs with acrylic paint, which won't break down. The white/cream areas on this screen show repairs made with acrylic paint.*

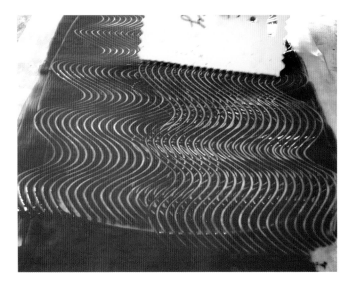

Drawing fluid spread on to an acrylic plate; a tiling blade is being used to lift out a design

Carefully place the screen on top of the etched filler to take a monoprint

Here, the filler has been spread on to an acrylic plate and sandwiched with another plate. When pulled apart, the filler generates amazing texture

Direct application of filler

If you find pulling screen filler across the screen difficult or stressful, you can put it on in other ways:

- *Draw on your design and paint around/outside it with filler to create positive imagery, or paint inside the design to create negative imagery.*
- *Stamp or print on filler, draw it on with a needle-nose bottle, dribble it on etc. Remember that direct application of this kind will print in the negative image.*
- *Apply the filler to a piece of plastic, etch into it and take a monoprint on to a screen. Note; this results in a very thin layer, so the screen may not last that long but this doesn't mean it's not worth doing. And you can always touch up with more screen filler.*

Cloth printed with a screen made from monoprinted screen filler

Using the screen

Designs made with screen filler can handle most media with the exception of bleach/chlorox. Bleach, coupled with boiling water are the agents used to remove the filler/design from the screen so don't use it as a discharge medium in this instance.

• Prepare your cloth according to the media you're using and pin or clamp it on to your print bench. Thickened dye paint, discharge paste or fabric paint will all work well, although fabric paint may cause the screen to deteriorate more quickly.
• Print with the screen using your chosen media and then wash it out (remember, don't let fabric paints dry out in the screen).
• Process and rinse the cloth according to the media you've used (see pages 61 to 69 for guidance).

Removing the design/filler

As already mentioned, screen filler creates a semi-permanent image on the screen. We say semi-permanent as over time, the filler will wear out, particularly if you've been using it with a lot of fabric paint, or with thickened dyes that have soda ash in them.

To guarantee removal of the filler, the screen must be reclaimed within 3 months of application. To remove it:

• Boil a kettle of water.
• Put on rubber gloves and a good mask. If you don't have a vapour mask, work outside in good ventilation.
• Place the screen in a sink or square container, flat/back side down. Pour bleach/chlorox all over it.
• Pour on boiling water and let things rest for a minute; back off at this point and be careful of inhaling bleach fumes (hence the mask) and don't get the bleach/boiling water on your skin as it will burn.
• Once the bleach/water mix has had 15 minutes or so to activate, start scrubbing the mesh vigorously. The screen filler should start to come out.
• If the filler proves resistant, rinse out the screen and repeat the bleach, boiling water and scrubbing process. Screens with designs on them of over 3 months old may prove stubborn or may resist re-claiming completely.
• Once the screen filler has been removed, rinse the screen under cold running water to remove all bleach. The screen mesh may be tinted a pale pink – this is residual staining left by the filler, so don't worry about it.
• Hold the screen up to the light – if any areas are still opaque, you'll need to repeat the re-claiming process.
• If the screen filler won't come out (totally), you'll have to create a new design by working around what's been left, or cut out the old mesh and replace it.

The cloth with its screen

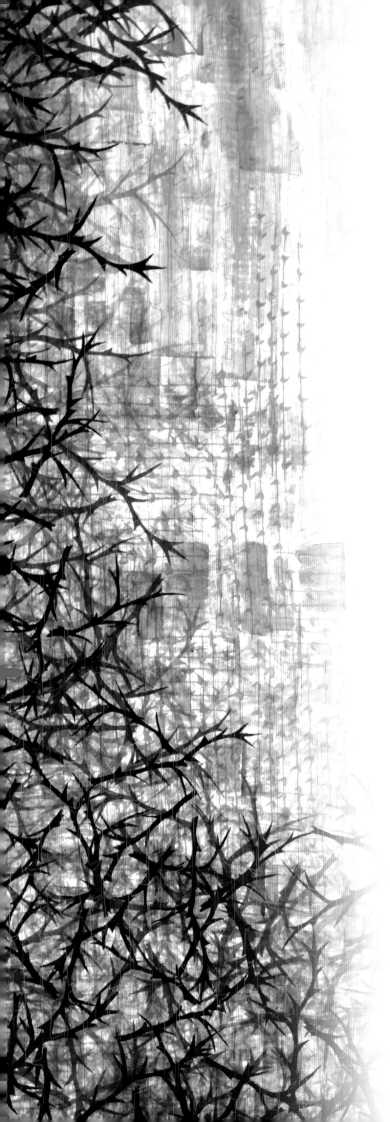

Creating Permanent Designs

Whilst this book is predominantly about the creation and use of temporary designs for the silkscreen, it seemed wrong not to include a simple way to create permanent designs. As you explore the potential of the screen, you'll probably discover imagery that you just can't live without, and which become part of your personal style. Acrylic paint will create a permanent, non-removable design that can be used with any media. The design is essentially painted or sprayed on and then left to dry; there's no need to use 'artist quality' acrylic, a cheap brand will do and it needs to be of a fairly heavy body consistency to minimise spread.

Generally speaking, we tend to test various approaches with temporary stencils first and if we like the outcome and believe we'll get a lot of use from it, we'll then create permanent screens.

Permanent paint screens can be used with any type of media, including thickened bleach/chlorox or bleach gel. Before use, we recommend applying masking tape to the back of the screen where the wood meets the mesh as the acrylic paint can crack at this joint and leak media.

When you've finished printing with a permanent screen, simply wash it out and let it dry – towel drying it will mean you can generally re-use it within 10 minutes or so.

Assemble the following:

- Silkscreen(s)
- A pot or tube of acrylic paint in a pale colour (avoid black)
- A can of spray acrylic
- A can of webbing spray
- Items to use as resists, including freezer paper, masking tape, bits of net, plastic moulding, construction tape etc.
- Paintbrushes and other tools to suit the design
- Sheet plastic or newspaper

PAINTED ACRYLIC

When painting on screen mesh with acrylic, acknowledge that you'll need to paint the design in about three times: working in several layers is better than trying to seal the mesh in one go. There are a couple of variations with this approach:

Painting around a drawn design using acrylic paint

Cut strips of masking tape have been stuck to the back of the screen prior to painting

Hand-painting positive images

- Trace or draw your design onto the inner (front) surface of your screen with a soft pencil. Drawing on the inner/front surface is important as the mesh will be flat on the table and you won't accidentally pierce it with the pencil, and lettering will be the correct way around.
- Now flip the screen over and paint around the design, remembering that where you apply paint, you'll seal the mesh. The open areas will be the printable areas. Leave the screen flat and let the first layer of paint dry, then paint over it again. You may need to do this a third time in order to seal the mesh.
- To check that the mesh is completely sealed, hold the screen up to the light. If you can see light coming through the paint, media will be able to come through these pinpricks too. Whilst this can create an interesting "dusting" effect, if you want a pure, clean image, apply another coat of paint.

Using resists to achieve positive imagery

- Make your design from torn or cut masking tape, freezer paper or cut contact paper.
- Apply it to the flat side/back of the screen.
- Keeping the screen back-side up, paint it. It doesn't matter if you go over the resist as you'll peel that off later. Always paint the screen from the back, never from both sides. If you paint from both sides, you'll seal the mesh behind the paper/plastic resist, which is what you want to keep open and free from paint. Again, it's better to apply several thin layers than attempt to seal the mesh in one go. Leave the screen to dry flat in between each layer.
- When the final layer of paint is dry and you're satisfied the mesh is sealed, peel off the resist.

Other direct application methods

Direct application gives the ability to create a negative image – what you'll ultimately print will be the space in-between the acrylic paint, not what you see in acrylic paint;

- Use brushes, needle-nose bottles, scrapers etc. to dribble, doodle or brush the acrylic paint straight on. Try 'printing' with leaves, fan brushes, corks etc.
- You can stand the screen upright and let the acrylic paint dribble down it (you'll need a thinner consistency paint for this to happen). Once you've got the runs you want, return the screen to a horizontal position to let the paint dry.
- Again, check for opacity but remember that free-fall applications will be hard to register when applying the second or third coat of paint to the screen.

SPRAY PAINTING

Instead of spray painting interfacing to create a screen stencil, you have the option of spraying the back of the screen. This will result in a screen with a permanent design on it, so make sure you like what you're about to do by practising on an interfacing stencil first!

• Ideally, work outside on a calm day (windy conditions make spraying difficult). Or, build yourself a spray booth out of an old cardboard box.

• Choose a stencil or an item to use as a resist; it might be something as fine as fruit cage netting, or plastic mesh, leaves, coins, string, sink liners, doilies, construction mesh, decorative plastic moulding etc.

• Lay the screen back/mesh side up on newspaper, and place the resist or stencil on top of it. You can use a water-soluble spray glue such as 505 to achieve a better bond but if the acrylic paint gets on to the glue, it may try to bond permanently, so do a test first. You can achieve some stability by taping stencils, string or mesh resists to the outer, wooden frame edge of the screen.

• The safest option is to simply let the stencil/resist lay on the mesh. With items such as fine netting, some spray will always blow under it even in calm conditions, so accept the free-fall of this design process!

• Spray on the acrylic paint by sweeping across the screen in a steady motion. Spray from above rather then from the side and don't over-apply, as too much spray paint may run and bleed under the resist. It's better to spray multiple layers, letting each one dry between applications.

• Keep the screen flat whilst the paint is drying.

• When you think you've sealed the exposed mesh, carefully pick the screen up, peer at it to see if you can see light coming through it. If light can penetrate the mesh, so can media, so keep adding more thin layers of spray paint.

Having said all of the above, you can choose to spray-paint without placing anything on the screen. Only apply one or two layers of paint; the tiny little holes/areas left by poor spray coverage will print interesting "dusting" or textural effects. You may also be able to find 'crackle' spray paint that's designed to split and crack once dry. We've had reasonable success with this.

Tile spacers have been placed on the screen to act as a resist before spraying

Spraying a screen with webbing spray; practise with the webbing spray on paper first!

WEBBING SPRAY

Once again, if you've made an interfacing stencil with webbing spray and love it, you have the choice of making a permanent screen with it. As this is a permanent design, you may want to practise again on paper first.

When you're ready to apply the webbing spray to a screen, lay out several sheets of newspaper and place the screen mesh-side up on the paper. Now spray the screen with the webbing spray (your test sprays will tell you how to work to get what you want). We find that between 3 and 5 applications are needed to create a decent textural effect but if you use the screen and wish you'd applied more webbing spray to it, wash it out after use, let it dry and spray it again.

And finally...

You may have heard of or even explored photo-emulsion screens. Whilst photo emulsion is the traditional method of generating a permanent design on a screen, we've chosen not to cover it for several key reasons:

- We don't have enough space in our studio for a darkroom or a decent-sized light-table, preferring to use all available space for large print tables.
- Whilst we have experience of the process, we personally find it messy and time consuming.
- The results can be unpredictable, particularly if the emulsion hasn't been stored correctly, or is old.
- We simply prefer other approaches!

However, if you'd like to learn more, then consult 'Complex Cloth' by Jane Dunnewold or chat to your favoured art/craft supplier about the Speedball range of photo-emulsion products.

Breakdown printed and over-dyed, then discharged using a permanent webbing spray screen

A selection of permanent spray-painted acrylic screens:

1. 'Crackle' spray paint
2. Plastic fern resist
3. Mesh resists
4. Webbing spray *(avoid black if you can)*
5. Mesh resists
6. Embriodery plastic resist
7. Plastic moulding resist

Media & Recipes

PROCION-TYPE MX DYES

The basic list of 'ingredients' for using Mx dyes as paints is;

• Procion-type Mx Dyes
• Sodium Carbonate/Soda Ash
• Urea (a wetting agent)
• Anti-oxidant (such as Ludigol or Resist Salt L)
• Water softener (such as Calgon)
• Manutex RS/Sodium Alginate (for making print paste)
• A rinsing agent such as Synthrapol or Metapex 38

Suppliers of these ingredients can be found in the Resources section.

Suitable Cloth for Mx Dyes

Procion-type Mx Dyes are formatted for use with cotton, linen, hemp, silk and viscose/rayon. They will not work on synthetic fibres such as nylon or polyester, nor are they effective with wool – even though wool is a natural fibre. Cellulose fibres such as cotton, linen, hemp and viscose/rayon will take a dye colour differently to protein fibres such as silk. In addition, different fabrics generate a different 'strike' or colour take-up.

Every type of cloth is different; some have fine fibres and others have heavy/thick fibres. Some are tightly woven whilst others have a loose weave structure. Let's take a brief look at this…

Tight weave vs a looser weave

Fine vs thick fibres; the Mx dye will react in the fibres once soda ash/sodium carbonate is added to the dye paint or is present in the cloth. Any type of individual fibre is only capable of holding so much dye – a fine fibre will hold less dye and saturate more quickly, a thick fibre will hold more dye and take longer to saturate. Jane Dunnewold suggests imagining the cloth as a car park capable of holding a finite number of cars. When the car park has reached its full capacity, no more cars (dye molecules) will be able to get in – the fibre will be fully saturated. To allow more cars in, you'd have to drive some out through a colour removal or discharge process. So, a very fine Silk Pongee/Habotai is a smaller car park than a heavy cotton velvet one and less dye will be needed to fill up the silk than the cotton.

Weave structure; a tightly woven fabric will mean that the dye paint has to work harder to get inside the fibres. A loosely woven fabric will be easier for the dyes to penetrate. Imagine different types of fencing; an open trellis will allow the elements through easily whereas a densely woven fence will make it harder for the wind and rain to penetrate. It's the same with a weave structure and what you're working with will have an impact on the crispness and depth of the marks achieved.

Note; we personally avoid using calico/muslin or other 'loomstate' fabrics for anything other than high-water immersion dyeing as it tends to 'push back' the dyes. If you choose to use calico/muslin or loomstate for the projects in this book, scour it very, very well and accept that it will take many processes and perseverance to get a decent depth of colour – but when you do get it, it can be fabulously rich.

As you work with dyes and different fabrics, it's always worth experimenting and making notes on the differences in dye strikes and colours. This means you'll be able to prepare dye paints that are right for the cloth and the colour saturation you're looking for… and you'll waste less dye because your quantities will be more accurate.

The Role of the Dye

The Mx dyes are your colouring agents (sorry to be obvious!). They're fibre-reactive and Soda Ash is the chemical used to drive the reaction between the dye and the fibre. They're at their most dangerous to health in their dry/powder state so wear a good quality mask when mixing significant quantities. Equally, wear gloves when handling the dyes and if they do get on your skin, don't use bleach to remove them. Instead, use a cleaner such as Reduran to get the worst off - the stains will fade after a couple of days.

Procion-type Mx dyes are classified as 'cold water' dyes but are manufactured to be used at a temperature of somewhere between 50-80°F, and will therefore need to be cured or 'batched' to aid striking.

If the dye paint is made without adding soda ash to it, it will last for up to 4 weeks if kept cool. Once soda ash is added to the dye paint, the chemical reaction will start to take place and the paint needs to be used within 4 to 8 hours. This is why we prefer to put the soda ash into the cloth, not the dye paint.

We source our dyes from Kemtex Educational Supplies and the list below shows the names and numbers as used by Kemtex at the time of writing. As a colour range we recommend two sets of basic primaries; 3 cold and 3 warm. Black and Dark Brown have been included to use as colours in their own right or to help you generate complex or dirtied colours and to darken/enrich the primaries;

Warm Primaries	Cold Primaries
Scarlet Red Mx-3G	Magenta Red Mx-8B
Royal Blue Mx-R	Bright Turquoise Mx-G
Golden Yellow Mx-3R	Acid Lemon Mx-8G
Kenactive Black K2647 and Dark Brown Mx-3G	

Feel free to invest in a larger colour range. Other good Kemtex colours include;

- Indigo Navy Mx-2G; a useful dark blue
- Red-Brown Mx-5BR; tea-rose in colour, Red-Brown is great for warming up Golden Yellow or enriching both Magenta and Scarlet
- Rust Orange (from the 'CD' range); not too dirty, this is a good 'warmer'
- Petrol Green (from the CD range); an attractive blue-green/green blue – depending on your perspective!

Many dye manufacturers produce pre-mixed colours that are 'pale' tints of something stronger, e.g. Pale Aqua is often drawn from something like Petrol Green. Think carefully before investing in these pale colours as they are often a poor economy. You can find pale tints by reducing the ratio of dye to print paste. Save your money and invest in colours that can be very difficult to find when you're starting out – such as neutrals.

How much dye to use is a tricky subject - because colour is subjective and different weights and types of cloth will respond differently to the same mixture of dye paint. Another key consideration is that some colours 'strike' faster and more aggressively than others. For example, we find that Magenta (cold red) is the fastest striker, whilst blues tend to be slow. Undertake specific experiments using our recipes as a starting point and adapt them to suit.

The Role of Soda Ash/Sodium Carbonate

Soda Ash or Sodium Carbonate is the chemical fixative needed to generate the chemical reaction with the dyes and fix them into the cloth. Once soda ash is added to a dye paint, the paint must be used up within 4 to 8 hours, depending on the climate you're working in.

We prefer to put the Soda Ash into our cloth, rather than our dyes as this means the dye paints will last – if kept cool – for up to 4 weeks. We have a soda 'vat' on the go at all times so it's ready when we want to soak cloth. If kept in a lidded bucket, the solution won't evaporate or go off. Wear a mask when mixing significant quantities of soda solution as the dry fine particles are hazardous if inhaled. This is the recipe we use;

- *3 tablespoons of soda ash per litre of water.*
- We tend to make up 10 litres at a time, which requires 450ml/g of soda ash, but 5 litres (which is about half a bucket and requires 225ml/g of soda ash) may be a better quantity for home use. It doesn't go off - just keep it covered so it doesn't evaporate.

Soda Ash doesn't like being dissolved in hot water, so start by putting the required amount of soda ash in a bucket, then add enough tepid water to get it dissolving. Top up with the required amount cold water.

Cloth soaking in the soda tubs; clean soda on the right, contaminated on the left for dyed cloth (which can bleed colour, even when well rinsed)

- Put your cloth in your soda-soaking tub and leave for between 10 and 20 minutes.
- Wring out/spin and work with it wet (more bleed) or wring/spin and line dry to work with it dry (crisper marks).
- If you have a stand-alone spin-dryer, collect the run-off soda solution and re-use it.
- We avoid tumble-drying soda-soaked fabric as a residue of soda tends to be left behind on the drum, and the effect of heat with soda may damage the cloth.
- Soda-soaked fabric can be stored for later use, but must be bone-dry. Silk will store for about a month whilst cotton, linen or viscose can be kept indefinitely. Note: don't store your dry, soda-soaked cloth folded; just stuff it into a bag or a box.

Warm Primaries

Golden Yellow

Scarlet

Royal Blue

Cold Primaries

Acid Yellow Lemon

Magenta

Turquoise

The ingredients for Chemical Water: Calgon (a water softener), Urea and Ludigol/Resist Salt L

Making print paste by using a hand-held electric mixer to beat in Sodium Alginate

Chemical Water

Chemical Water is the starting point for all dye paints. You can use chemical water that has Urea, water softener and an anti-oxidant in it, or a simplified version that just has Urea. Let's look at these 3 chemicals/agents;

- *Urea* is a hydroscopic or wetting agent that constantly attracts moisture to itself from the environment. As such, it keeps the dye paints from drying out too quickly. The quantity needed depends on environmental conditions; Bob Adams doesn't use it at all as he works in a very humid climate. Other artists who work in very dry, arid conditions may use double the amount we do.
- A *water softener* such as Calgon is necessary in areas that have very hard water as hard water can affect the colour strike.
- An *anti-oxidant* such as Ludigol or Resist Salt L is useful where air or water pollution may affect the dye colours.

Whatever combination of ingredients you end up using, it's still chemical water and it can be convenient to have it ready to hand. Stored cool, it will keep indefinitely and volume quantities are:

Warm Water	Urea	Ludigol	Calgon
5 litres	500ml / 400-500g	25ml	25ml
10 litres	1000ml / 800-900g	50ml	50ml
As a rough guide, 50ml urea = 35g weighed. In hot, dry weather, increase the quantity of Urea by approximately 15-20% to prevent the dye paints drying out too quickly.			

Print Paste

A thickening agent (Sodium Alginate/Manutex RS) is added to the Chemical Water to make a thick Print Paste. Dye is added to this paste mixture to create a consistency that's suitable for screen printing and many other direct surface applications.

We usually make about 4 litres at a time and keep it in the fridge, where it will last for about 4 weeks. If you've got some that's been hanging around for longer than this, it may smell of ammonia and have gone off. Dyes can still take well with old paste (although the colour can be less intense), but if you want to be sure, mix a new batch.

However much you make at a time, you can mix by hand, use an old Magimix or better still, a hand-held electric mixer. We mix a thicker-than-usual print paste that has a 'dropping' rather than a running consistency as it's more suitable for processes such as Breakdown Printing, and is easily thinned by beating more Chemical Water into it. Volume quantities are:

Chemical Water	Sodium Alginate/Manutex RS
1 litre	45ml / 30-35g
2 litres	90ml / 65-70g
4 litres	190ml / 130g

If mixing by hand or with a hand-held electric mixer, put the required amount of Chemical Water into a tub, start mixing and sprinkle on the Sodium Alginate/Manutex RS as you mix.

Mix thoroughly for about 3 minutes and then leave in a cool place for at least 4 hours to thicken up, ideally overnight.

Making Dye Paints

As mentioned before, we generally prefer to put the soda in the fabric rather than in the dyes. There are several reasons for this;

- The dyes last longer as there's no soda for them to bond with.
- We've observed that silk screens that have a semi-permanent design on them of screen filler can break down more quickly when used with dyes that have soda in them. We suspect the repeated pulling of soda-dyes sets up an abrasive reaction that breaks down the screen filler.
- Processes such as 'Breakdown Printing' need dyes without soda in them, as the prepared screens will often take all day to dry.

When working with cloth where you want to keep a white (or very pale) background, consider switching to the soda-in-dye method. It can be hard to keep a white background as it's difficult to avoid staining even with cold-water rinsing (particularly when Magenta dye is present). Soda-in-dye means that the areas of white cloth you've left un-touched have no soda in them, so staining is less likely.

Different Mx dye colours can strike more quickly and more aggressively than others. We tend to compensate for this when making dye paints by using 'skinny' or 'fat' teaspoons. For example, reds and yellows (and therefore oranges) generally strike faster than blues and blacks…

- *Black;* when mixing black, you may want to consider doubling the dye quantity to get a 'true' black.
- *Turquoise;* blues and blacks strike more slowly than yellows, reds or oranges, Turquoise can sometimes be particularly sluggish, so consider increasing the amount of dye by half or using 'fat' measures to help it keep up with faster bed-fellows.
- *Yellow;* when mixing yellow, consider increasing the quantity by half or using a 'fat' measure. Whilst it strikes fairly quickly, yellow is easily contaminated by other colours.
- *Magenta;* the fastest, most aggressive striker of them all, consider using 'skinny' measures.

How much dye you put into your paint mixture is dependent on you – the more dye, the more intense the colour. Equally, the type of fabric you're using will determine the colour strength; fine silk fibres need less dye than cottons and linens. A good starting point is to mix up a fairly strong mixture and reduce the colour strength as you need to by adding more Print Paste. The following recipe will make a quarter-litre (250ml - about 8 fl oz) of paint. Dyes in our studio are always mixed to this recipe/strength, and weakened with print paste as required.

- **Put a little warm water in a container twice the size of the volume of paint you're making; you'll be stirring vigorously!**
- **Add 2 (plump) teaspoons of Mx dye powder and stir well to dissolve.**
- **Now top up to 250ml / 8 fl oz with Print Paste.**
- **Beat the mixture well until it's smooth.**

Dissolving the dye in a little warm water

Adding print paste to the dissolved dye

Mx dyes will gradually bond with water at warmer temperatures, so their shelf life is limited once mixed. Shelf life can be prolonged by keeping the mixtures in the fridge (covered), but it can be risky to use them after 4 weeks and there's no guarantee on results.

Ultimately, the results depend on dye quantities, fibre types, curing/fixing time and curing temperature (warmer is better!) - you'll need to experiment and/or undertake samples. The more you practise, the more you'll engage with the process and understand it. Ultimately, you'll establish what dye strength is needed to achieve the result you're looking for on the cloth you're using.

Curing/Batching Thickened Dye Paints

In addition to soda ash (which is already in the cloth, or the dye paint), three other 'ingredients' or conditions are required to maximise the dye/fibre reaction:

Moisture:	Almost dry to the touch or very wet
Heat:	15°C - 35°C (60°F - 85°F)
Time:	4 hours as a minimum, overnight or up to 24 hours

This process is often referred to as curing or batching.

Rolling dye-printed cloth in plastic before batching

Moisture

Dye molecules can penetrate fibre more effectively when moisture is present, although the amount of moisture can be so little that the fabric can feel almost dry to the touch. If the fabric has dried out very quickly or become bone dry to the touch, the reaction will stop, so avoid drying fabric in direct sunlight, drying it too much or too quickly. You can retain moisture content by using plastic sheeting (cover the fabric with it or roll it up). We prefer to let pieces dry off a little before rolling in plastic, as we hate washing plastic! If your cloth does get too dry and you're worried about a good strike, lay it on plastic and re-hydrate it by spraying lightly with Chemical Water. Then roll it up.

Heat

Cure between 15°C - 35°C (60°F - 85°F). If the temperature's too cold, the reaction of the dye is slowed down or even halted completely. To hot and it may dry too quickly for proper curing.

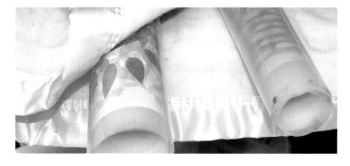

In the winter or cold weather, we use an electric blanket to provide the heat required for the batching proces

In the summer, or if the studio is heated overnight, let the cloth sit overnight, curing gradually in or under plastic. In winter or in an un-heated studio, roll it up in plastic sheeting (very wet or almost-dry) before sliding the tubes in between a folded electric blanket, set to the highest temperature to provide even background heat. If you can't get hold of an old electric blanket, bring the pieces indoors and place them somewhere warm – under (but not on top of) a radiator will do - and cure for a longer period.

Rolling when wet may cause colours to bleed and blend (which can be fantastic). If you want to keep colours separate, or keep very crisp marks and lines, don't cover or roll when very wet - let the piece semi-dry then cover or roll in plastic and cure in a heated room or in an electric blanket.

Time

Allow 4 hours as a minimum or ideally overnight for curing, as the dye needs time to react with the fibre molecules. Our standard curing time is 12-18 hours/overnight (and we find it exciting to get rinsing the next morning!). If you can't get decent heat for the curing process, let things sit in plastic for 24 hours to give the dyes a better chance to strike.

Rinsing

If you can, use a rinsing agent such as Synthrapol/Metapex 38 as it will 'trap' dye particles and help prevent colour contamination. You'll need a few drops to a half teaspoon when hand-rinsing, and up to 1 teaspoon for a full load when machine washing – it all depends on the size of the load and the heaviness of the fibre. If you don't have a rinsing agent use a mild detergent suitable for delicates or woollens.

* Rinse off excess dye in **cold** water and a rinsing agent in a bucket, changing the water regularly.
* Machine wash **cold** with a rinsing agent, once or possibly twice if an aggressive colour (e.g. Magenta) is present.
* Machine wash again in warm water with a rinsing agent at 40-60°C.

If you wash in hot water too quickly, excess dye particles may transfer and cause staining (although the use of a rinsing agent will help to prevent this). Remember – the stronger the colours/the more dye you've used, the more washes you'll need. If we know we're taking the cloth on to another dye or discharge process that will subsequently entail more washing, we normally hand rinse cold, machine rinse cold and then carry on with the next wet process.

Sometimes the sodium alginate/Manutex RS in the thick dye paints can be difficult to remove. This can happen if the dye paint has dried out too fast (e.g. the cloth has been hung to dry in direct sunlight). If this does happen, do the following:

* Dissolve 1-3 tablespoons of soda in hot (about 60°C) water. The amount of soda is dependent on the amount of cloth, but we find that 3 tablespoons handles a large piece of cloth.
* Add a drop of rinsing agent.
* Give the piece a good mashing in the bucket, then leave to soak for between 10 and 30 minutes, mashing occasionally.
* Rinse out by hand in warm to hot water.
* Do a final warm/hot (40-60°C) water rinse by machine.

If the sodium alginate/Manutex RS still hasn't shifted, repeat the process.

Back-Staining

Back-staining is a method of tinting any white/unprinted areas of cloth with half-exhausted dyes. It can be risky and it'll take some practise to accurately forecast what colour of tint you'll get.

The principle of back-staining is to acknowledge that there may be some semi-active dye present in the cloth after batching. The intention is to use it - with the help of hot water and additional soda-ash - to colour any white areas of cloth. To proceed:

- Dissolve 3 tablespoons of soda ash in some warm water in a bucket.
- Half-fill the bucket with hot water (about 60°C – it should feel hot, but not uncomfortable through your gloves).
- Add the printed cloth (do not rinse it first).
- Mash and pound the cloth to help the excess or semi-active dye to release itself into the water.
- Leave the fabric, in this bucket, for at least 30 minutes and up to 4 hours.
- Then rinse the cloth as usual.

When first attempting back-staining, avoid doing it with something you think you're going to love, as there is a risk things could go wrong. The colour of the tint you'll get will depend on the dye colours present in the cloth, and how active they might be. And remember, the fact that individual colours strike differently will also have an effect on the resulting tint.

If you're dealing with yardage and want to back-stain it, put the fabric into the washing machine and add 3 tablespoons of soda ash. Run the machine on a hot wash (60°C). When the cycle has finished, run the machine again at 40-60°C to get rid of any lingering traces of dye.

The left hand side shows the back-stained cloth. The right hand piece of cloth was rinsed 'correctly'

DISCHARGE PASTE

Discharge chemicals are used to remove colour from cloth. They won't work on all types of dyed fabrics, so testing first is important. Turquoise Mx dye is usually resistant to discharge, so always test any fabric you have containing turquoise.

Mx dyed cloth or commercial discharge cloth are normally discharged with either:

• Jacquard Discharge Paste, available ready-mixed
• Formosol powder/crystals
• Thiourea Dioxide (Thiox) powder/crystals

We choose to make our own discharge paste using Formosol as we find it cheaper and more effective.

Formosol Discharge

Formosol will discharge Mx dyed cellulose fibres and silk, but not wool.

Wear a mask when handling Formosol in powder format and when steam ironing to activate it. The powder will oxidise and lose strength when in contact with the air, so decant into smaller tubs as you use it.

Formosol is activated by heat and steam and can be mixed with print paste, water or a combination of both to get different consistencies. Always work in a well- ventilated area and/or wear a good quality mask.

The basic ratio is 1 part Formosol to 10 parts 'carrying' agent; which can be plain water, Chemical Water or Print Paste. This ratio makes a fairly strong solution, but it's strength can be reduced by adding more print paste. To mix 500ml /16fl oz of paste:

1. **Dissolve 50g (3 generous tablespoons) of Formosol in a little warm (but not hot) water to make a runny paste.**
2. **Top up with 500ml of print paste and beat well with a hand-mixer.**
3. **Store covered, in the fridge or somewhere cool.**

To print and activate Formosol:

1. *Pin out your dry, coloured cloth (it should not have been soda soaked).*
2. *Print using discharge paste and your chosen screen. When you've finished printing, let the cloth dry on the bench, or hang it up.*

3. *When the Formosol paste is completely dry, use a steam iron set to cotton to activate it. The iron is a tool and the way you use it will effect the results you get; the more you steam the more the paste activates. The less you steam the less the paste activates. As such, you can achieve varying shades of discharge by using the iron creatively. Always work in a well-ventilated area and wear a suitable mask.*
4. *Sun activation; you can also experiment by activating the paste with sunlight. Having printed on the paste, hang the piece in direct sunlight; as it dries it will slowly discharge. We've had great results using sunlight and it avoids the fumes. However, do test this approach as generally speaking, the colour and depth of discharge will be different when using sunlight rather than the steam iron.*

Whether you've activated by steam or sunlight, rinse the cloth well after activation by hand or machine. If the dried-in paste proves stubborn to remove, wash in hot water with some soda ash added to it.

Note: Formosol does not have to be mixed with print paste. It can be mixed with water and used for spray-discharge or painting. The ratio is the same; dissolve 50g/3 tbsp of Formosol in a little warm water. Top up to 500ml with cold water. Store in a lidded jar and keep it cool. Formosol-in-water can also be mixed with Formosol paste to create runnier consistencies suitable for needle-nose bottles, painting, and spattering. We usually have Discharge Paste and Discharge Liquid ready to use in our studio.

Jacquard Discharge Paste

Jacquard Discharge paste is a pre-mixed colour removing paste. Jacquard makes the only available 'off the shelf' product and it is suitable for cotton, linen, viscose (rayon) and silk, but results can be dubious on wool. It can be used straight from the tub, which makes it easily accessible, but more expensive. It can be made to go further by mixing it with Print Paste; up to a 50:50 ratio. It's activated by heat and steam. Read the instructions, but you may find that you get a better result if you activate it damp (not wet) rather than dry.

FABRIC PAINTS & ACRYLICS

There are many water-based paints available on the market. Here are a couple of pointers to help you understand the various choices:

- Paints are available ready-mixed in translucent (e.g. see through) colours, opaque colours and metallics.
- All fabric paints are related to acrylic paints. The difference lies in the formula of the paint. All paint has a binder, which is the polymer part. The colour comes from the addition of pigment - the pure colour. Fabric paints also tend to have softeners, surfactants (wetting agents) and other ingredients in them to make the paints more sheer and to reduce the impact on the hand of the fabric. This is easily tested; just paint or print a piece of fabric using an acrylic and a good quality fabric paint; nine times out of ten, the acrylic paint will dry to a stiffer hand.
- Most fabric paints (and acrylics) are very light fast, far more so than Mx dyes. The good brands provide data sheets showing the performance of different colours.

A simple way of looking at polymer paint products is to consider two key continuums:

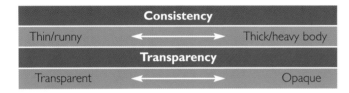

Consistency		
Thin/runny	← →	Thick/heavy body
Transparency		
Transparent	← →	Opaque

Generally speaking, the C2C studio uses printable consistency, transparent/translucent paints, although metallics veer towards the opaque as the mica that creates the sparkle also creates a level of opacity.

General Information

- Fabric paints are water-based pigment products that *coat the surface* of the fabric rather than penetrating and reacting with it (as in the case of Procion-type MX dyes). As such, they are suitable for use with both natural and synthetic fibres. Fabric paints have usually had a surfactant added to them to reduce the impact of the paint on the hand of the fabric.
- Textile 'screen inks' are another name for printable fabric paints. They usually contain a drying retardant to reduce the potential of the paint drying in your screen and sealing the mesh.
- Fabric paints can be bought translucent or opaque and can usually be mixed together to create different levels of translucency (this is usually true when using a single brand, but do test when mixing different brands). Metallics can also be mixed with ordinary colours to generate lustrous effects.
- Fabric paint can be made more transparent by mixing it with (Transparent) Extender Base. This is the binder the pigment has been suspended in and increasing the amount of base to pigment will increase the transparency.
- Most fabric paints require heat to set them. Acrylics aren't designed to be washed, but are okay if heat set.
- Fabric paint will stiffen the hand of the fabric but often, the hand is returned back to normal after the fabric has been heat set and washed.

- If you use Mx dyes on cloth subsequent to using fabric paints, the integrity of the paint colour will depend on the opacity of the fabric paint; sheer or transparent colours will be affected the most.

A selection of fabric paints, with transparent extender base

Guidelines on Use

- **Do not** use fabric paints on cloth that has been pre-soaked in soda.
- You can work on ironed or un-ironed fabric; un-ironed can add nice texture.
- You can work on dry fabric, wet-on-wet or wet-on-damp.
- The paints can be applied through the usual surface application techniques (painting, dragging, stamping, monoprinting etc.) and can be used through a silk-screen – but never let the paints dry out in the screen; wash up immediately on finishing.
- You can build up layers of fabric paint without heat-setting each layer. Working wet-on-wet can achieve great results but in a similar manner to dye, the true results may not be apparent until the paint has settled into the cloth and is dry.
- On a sunny day, hang the piece in direct sunlight and it'll dry in a jiffy… but never use paints in direct sunlight, as they'll dry out very fast in the screen or tool and ruin them.
- One point worth noting is that fabric paint that's stitched and then un-picked will leave holes that won't close (even with washing), which could be a feature – or not.

Cloth over-printed with gold fabric paint

Heat Setting

It's always a good idea to follow the manufacturers' instructions, but generally speaking, the following principles apply:

- Once the paint has been applied and dried, 'air-cure' for 12-24 hours before heat setting. This will allow a better bond with the surface of the cloth.
- All fabric paints require heat-setting if they are to be washed, and we always heat set even if the piece is unlikely to be washed. To heat-set, simply iron the cloth using parchment and a dry iron, set to somewhere between the wool and cotton setting. Work with the fabric right side up, using a pressing cloth or baking parchment to avoid paint/ink transfer onto the iron and to prevent scorching. Whilst we all hate ironing, don't skimp – follow the manufacturers' instructions on timing and iron settings. We usually flip the cloth over and repeat the process from the back (belt and braces!).

Once the fabric paint has been set, your fabric can be washed, but this isn't a pre-requisite. We don't normally wash until about a week after heat-setting to really allow the paint to settle. Often, any stiffening of the hand of the cloth is returned back to normal after setting and washing.

Acrylics

Acrylic paints were designed for use on paper, board or canvas and are available in a variety of consistencies, all of which can be altered based on what you want to accomplish. Just because the manufacturer didn't envision the paint being used on fabric doesn't mean you can't co-opt it.

As with fabric paints, you get what you pay for. Trying to save money by buying 'school' or 'student quality' acrylics is often a misplaced economy. These lower-grade products generally have less pigment in them and the polymer binders aren't such a high spec. Buy the best quality you can afford. Some great brands include:

- *Golden*
- *Liquitex*
- *Lascaux*
- *Tri-Art*

All of the colours can be extended with water or added to the vast range of available mediums. They can also be used 'a la prima' (straight out of the bottle/tube), but this will work out expensive and is probably best saved for final accents, or when you've practised!

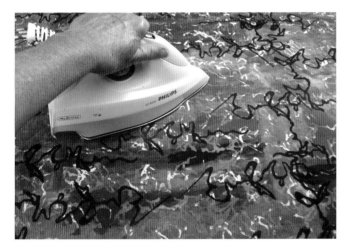

Heat setting

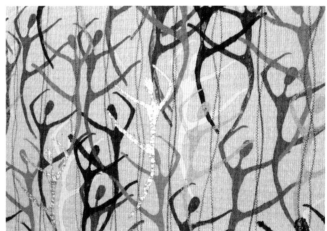

Cloth printed with acrylic and accents of metal leaf

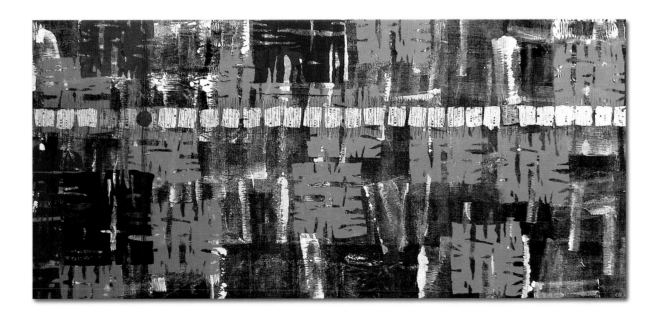

Colour Mixing

Colour is very subjective; one person's burgundy is another person's plum. As such, the colour recipes provided here are to our personal descriptions, and may not match what you see in your head. If so, re-label them in a way that makes sense to you. What we discuss in this section is relevant whether you're using thickened dye paints or fabric paints.

The results you'll get when mixing cold colours together vs warm colours will be quite different. For example;

Cold mixes;
- Lemon Yellow & Magenta will give you a bright, brilliant, 'acid' orange.
- Lemon Yellow and Turquoise will make a brilliant, sparky emerald green.
- Turquoise & Magenta will give you a bright, sparky purple.

Warm mixes;
- Golden Yellow & Scarlet will give you a warm, rich orange.
- Golden Yellow & Royal Blue will give you a dirty green… not quite olive, but almost.
- Royal Blue & Scarlet will give you a plummy purple.

Mixing Proportions

Ultimately, the best way to learn about colour and colour mixing is to get stuck in with the paints. The first rule of thumb is never assume that the way a dye colour looks in the pot or when wet on the fabric is the way it'll look once rinsed and dried. This is a tricky thing for your eyes and your head to manage, but will come with practice and observation. As you work, consider making a record on paper with a note of the colours used, in what proportions and combinations. Equally, tear off little bits of cloth from your experiments and glue them into a reference book as this will give you a truer record of the way the different mixtures work on cloth.

When mixing, you'll get different results depending on the proportion of colours used, for example;

- A mix of Lemon Yellow & Magenta where the proportion of yellow is greater than Magenta will give you a bright Yellow-Orange.
- A mix of Lemon Yellow & Turquoise where the proportion of yellow is greater than Turquoise will give you a bright lime – or yellowy – green.
- A mix of Turquoise and Magenta where the proportion of turquoise is greater than magenta will give you a bright blue-violet.
- A mix of Golden Yellow and Scarlet where the proportion of scarlet is more than the golden yellow will give you a warm, red-orange.
- A mix of Golden Yellow and Royal Blue where the proportion of golden yellow is greater than the royal blue will give you a warm, yellowy green.
- A mix of Royal Blue and Scarlet where the proportion of scarlet is greater than the proportion of royal blue will give you a reddish-plum.

So, you need to think about what colours you're trying to achieve. Are you looking for cold, bright, high-energy colours? If so, explore the cold primaries. Are you looking for rich, muted, warm colours? If so, explore the warm primaries. Then try mixing cold colours with warm colours to find out what else you can achieve.

Complex Colours

We define a complex colour as a colour that's been adulterated to make a 'dirtier' version of itself. The key principle is to adulterate the colour by adding a smidge of its complementary colour. The complementary 'couplings' are:

Primary Colour		Complementary
Red	⟶	Green
Yellow	⟶	Purple
Blue	⟶	Orange
Secondary Colour		**Complementary**
Green	⟶	Red
Purple	⟶	Yellow
Orange	⟶	Blue

For example, to mix ochre;

- Start with Golden Yellow (warm yellow). Bit by bit, add purple until the golden yellow had turned to the ochre you see in your head.
- As you have two reds (warm and cold) and two blues (warm and cold) in your colour palette to make that Purple, there's room to find plenty of ochres. You could also choose to use Brown as the dirtying agent, so try different approaches.

When mixing any complex colour, the end result is always subjective to the proportions you use, for example;

- To mix a complex secondary, start by mixing equal parts of the two primaries required and then add a half-part of the complementary. Or…
- Mix the secondary using equal parts of the primaries required and then add the complementary colour bit-by-bit until you get the exact shade of complex secondary you want.

These different approaches will produce a never-ending range of complex colours and that's the magic of it all! Here are some suggestions to play with based on the Mx dye paint colours mentioned earlier;

- *Rust Orange;* try equal parts of Warm Yellow & Warm Red to make the Orange. Add approximately a half part of Turquoise, or for a different rust orange, substitute Turquoise for Royal Blue.
- *Olive Green;* mix equal parts Warm Yellow and Warm Blue and then add (up to a half part) of Cold Red (Magenta) or Warm Red (Scarlet). Or, add Black bit by bit to Warm Yellow.
- *Chestnut Brown;* 1 part Golden Yellow, half parts each of Scarlet and Royal.
- *Petrol Green;* 1 part Cold Blue (Turquoise), a smidge of Black and a smidge of Cold Yellow (Acid Lemon). Experiment with your 'smidge' amounts.

We also use Black & Brown as agents for generating dark, rich colour effects. We use Black as the darkening agent for blues and reds and Brown as the darkening agent for yellows and reds. We make this decision based on the fact that the Kenactive Black dye we use has a blue/green undertone. If it's used with the yellows, you'll get greens - great greens but certainly not ochre! If it's used to darken magenta you'll get a pinkish maroon whilst if you darken magenta with brown you will get a deep, rich red. Try the following mixes;

- *Rich Claret;* 2 parts Scarlet, 1 part Magenta, a half part of Black. Or, try 2 parts Magenta, 1 part Scarlet and a half part of black (fiddle with the proportions of black).
- *Blood;* try 2 parts Scarlet, 1 part Magenta and up to 1 part Dark Brown.
- *Dried Blood;* try 2 parts Scarlet, 2 parts Dark Brown. You may want to add some Magenta.
- *Aubergine;* try 2 parts Scarlet, 1 part Magenta, a half part Dark Brown and a half part Black (and try switching the Scarlet and Magenta proportions and fiddling with the Black and Brown proportions).

The permutations are infinite and fiddling with the proportions is one of life's great joys! Ultimately it's important to remember that we all see and describe colours differently. The kind of terracotta, olive, aubergine, ruby, chestnut, ochre, rust orange, plum that you're seeking will be different to someone else's. As such, you need to experiment with proportions until you get the colour you want. Having got it – make a note of how you got it or commit it to memory. Or just have fun trying to find it again!

Rust Orange
1 Golden Yellow
1 Scarlet
½ Turquoise
or
1 Golden Yellow
1 Scarlet
½ Royal Blue

Olive Green

Chestnut

Petrol Green

Complex colours achieved by using a smidge of complemntaries

Rich Claret

Blood

Dried Blood

Aubergine

Some results achieved by using Brown and Black to 'murk up' reds

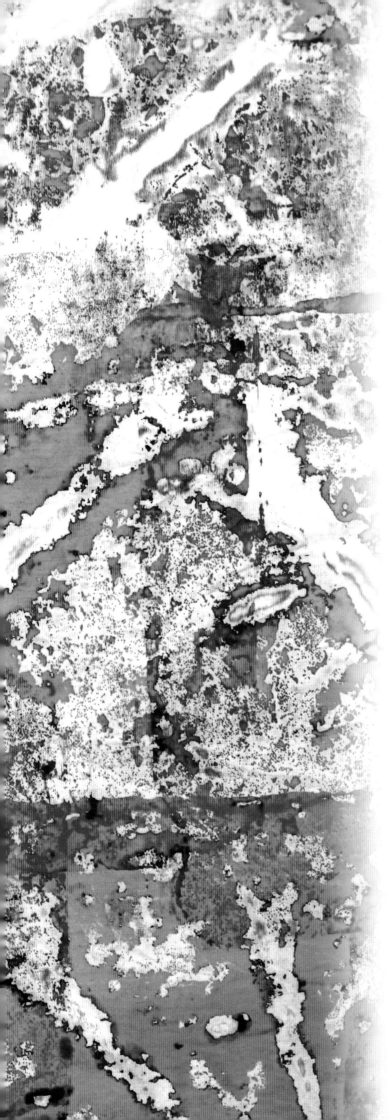

Re-meshing a Screen

Accidents happen – you accidently pierce the mesh of a screen. Or you decide it's time to move on from permanent designs you've made in acrylic paint. Either way, it's time to re-mesh the screen. Whilst you'll never get the same tension as a manufactured screen, with a bit of effort and a good staple gun you can get perfectly acceptable stretch. If you've water-proofed the screen with tape, try to get most of it off. If it won't come off, then simply cut out the mesh along the inner rim of the frame. You'll be left with an empty wooden frame.

You now have a choice:

• Invest in screen mesh (woven polyester, 43T/10xx)
OR
• Use polyester curtain sheer

When re-meshing, some people prefer to work opposite sides of the frame, We don't, so the approach described below is our preferred method. Experiment and find out what works best for you. Whatever route you choose, we recommend firing in the staples at a slight angle rather than straight up or down. This can help to prevent runs along the weave.

1. *Remove the existing mesh.*

2. *Cut a piece of new mesh/sheer about 5cm/2" larger than the frame (you'll need the excess to grab hold of).*

3. *Place the frame on a table and position the mesh/sheer evenly on top.*

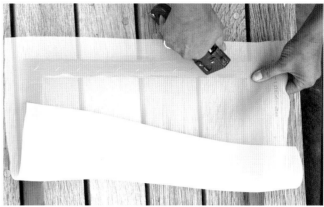

4. *Starting at a corner, use a staple gun to fire in the first staple (at an angle). Then, tension the mesh at the opposite end and fire in staples until you've reached the next corner. Try to keep the straight edge of the mesh aligned with the straight edge of the screen and staple every 2.5cm/1".*

5. *Now move to the right or left of the side you've just stapled (not opposite). Tension the mesh/sheer (as tightly as you can) and fire in staples along this second frame edge until you've reached the next corner.*

6. *Now move to one of the remaining two sides and repeat the process but this time, you be applying tension across the width of the screen to the opposite side, as well as along the edge. As such, you'll tension then staple, tension then staple and so forth until you reach the end of the third frame edge.*

7. *Finally, move to the remaining side of the frame. Again, tension up in two directions - away from the corner and against the opposite side; tension then staple, tension then staple until you've reached the end of the fourth side of the frame.*

8. *At this stage, we like to put a few reinforcing staples at each corner, then hammer all of the staples to make sure they're firmly sunk into the wooden frame. Trim off the excess mesh.*
- *If appropriate, use tape to waterproof the wooden frame again.*
- *Voila, you have a home-stretched screen that will do a good job for you.*

Projects - Building Experience Through Exploration

We wanted to include some 'projects' to help you build experience and encourage you to explore. Just like any other skill, screen printing can take time to master and you'll need to practise and suspend judgement on your early results. We've also observed that students have a tendency to stop 'layering' too soon. Knowing when to stop is challenging and ultimately, the only way forward is to push things a little and see what happens.

However, it's important to stress that layering multiple wet processes doesn't happen all at once. If you're working with thickened dye paints, the soda present in the cloth will only be capable of handling a finite quantity of dye. As such, the cloth will need to be batched, rinsed, dried and re-soaked in soda for the next process. It can take many days – and sometimes weeks – to build layer upon layer. And in between processes, it's important to iron your work-in-progress, pin it up and really look at it. When trying to decide on your next move, consider the following:

- *Visual interest:* visual interest is often driven through the use of contrasting elements. Contrast can be achieved through colour, value, texture, shape, line and so forth.
- *A sense of cohesion:* whilst contrast is important and can range from the subtle to the garish, it's important that design and compositional elements have a sense of belonging and have relationship with each other. Just as with contrast, relationships can be driven through the use of value, colour, scale, texture, line and shape. So for example, you may be driving contrast using a change of scale by adding a larger design element to the piece, but that element could be a larger version of a shape already present in the cloth… which will build relationship at the same time.
- *Background & Perspective:* generally speaking, we observe that students find it easier to start building background before tackling the foreground or the strong compositional elements. Take a look at the cloth and ask yourself; "am I done with the background yet, does the background have enough depth and interest?". If so, start planning the foreground element(s) of the piece.
- *Colour;* Colour use is important when building contrast and relationship. For example, you can work in a close colour range, in a monochromatic theme or in high contrast compositions using complementary colours.
- *Value:* varying a single colour from light to dark can create shadows, movement and depth.
- *Transparency;* use pale value dye paint mixtures or transparent fabric paints to achieve subtle elements and to allow what's beneath to gleam through. Discharge can also achieve this for you.
- *Opacity;* use opaque fabric paints to generate contrast, beef up impact and to emphasise a sense of an image being 'on top' or obviously foreground.
- *Imagery;* what addition will move the piece forward? Think line, texture and shape. Relationship is key.
- *Scale;* what size imagery works best? Do you need to include a range of different sizes of mark? This is particularly important if you're trying to develop a sense of perspective.

So, lots for you to think about. In the meantime, try having a go at some or all of the following 'projects' to get you started. For simplicity, we've based most of the exercises on thickened dye paints and/or discharge. You can of course use fabric paints but acknowledge that the hand of the cloth will change, particularly with multiple layering. Refer to the recipes on pages X to Y to make the paints or discharge paste. And remember, for any of these exercises, you don't have to use primaries. Try creating more complex colours using the recipes provided.

Before you start, prepare your cloth by scouring it and soda soaking it. We'd recommend you try these exercises on dry cloth and move on to experiment with printing on damp or wet cloth if you want to explore the impact of bleed. From time to time, vary the size and shape of your cloth; the format could be square, rectangular or very long and thin, but work on something of a reasonable size.

We suggest you follow the exercises fairly closely to begin with as we've observed that the learning tends to be easier. Having done them, you can take things further by mixing different elements of different exercises together. When you get to this stage, the key question to keep asking is "what if..?". Try making a note of what you think will happen, then undertake your experiment and see if you were right. But don't worry if you weren't – that's what experimentation is all about – learning and discovering.

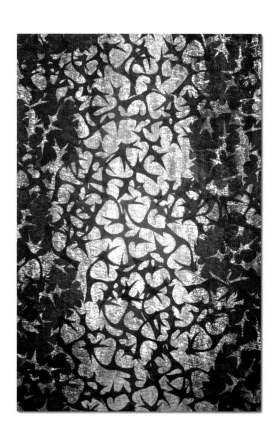

Line into Texture

This exercise allows you to explore how a simple line design can create texture if heavily over-printed.

- Pin out your cloth.
- Mix a single colour of thickened dye paint. You'll be printing with one colour, in one value.
- Print the line design at least three times, all over the cloth, remembering to work off the edges.
- You may need to print as many as six layers; keep looking at what you're achieving, remembering that the purpose of this exercise is to generate texture by printing with simple line imagery.
- Batch the cloth, rinse it, iron it and then pin it up to consider it.

As a variation, try this exercise using two close or analogous colours (e.g. yellow and orange, orange and red, blue and purple etc.).

Texture/Background from Shape

This exercise will allow you to explore how background can be created by over-printing a shape. We suggest you start by working with a single colour, but add print paste to it to bring the value down lightly; we suggest a ratio of either equal parts dye paint to print paste or one part dye paint to half a part print paste.

Chose a shape-based design; it could be organic (e.g. a leaf, a squiggle) or geometric (e.g. a square, rectangle, rhomboid). The edges of the shape could be crisp (e.g. straight-edged) or rough (e.g. torn edge). Pin out your dry, soda-soaked cloth and then:

- Print the shape imagery all over the cloth, remembering to work off the edges. For this first layer, don't overlap the prints.
- If working with a 'regular' shape (e.g. one with fairly even sides), try printing a repeat in rows or try turning the screen and printing at angles.
- Now print the image again. If you've printed in rows the first time, do this again but go 'in between' the first set of rows. If you've printed randomly and changed the angle of the screen, continue to do so.
- Now consider the result and decide if you want to print a third layer.
- Batch, rinse, iron and pin up the cloth to consider the results.

Variations on this exercise might include using one colour, but in two values or using analogous colours such as red and yellow, blue and purple etc.

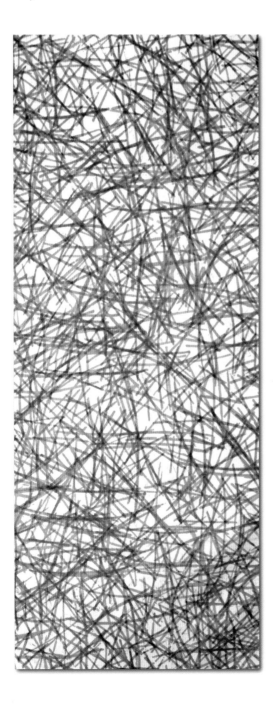

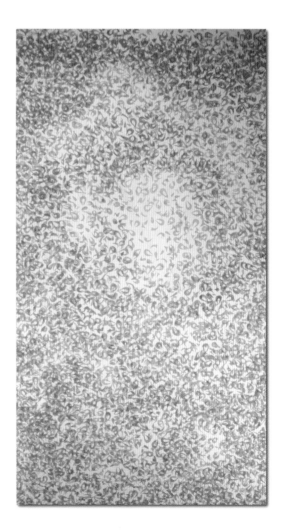

Layering Value

This exercise involves printing the cloth three times with three different values of a single colour, moving from pale, to medium to dark. Pick the imagery you want to use; it could be textural, line or shape-based, organic or geometric etc.

- Choose a colour you wish to use for the background, and make 250ml as a thickened dye paint. This will be your strongest value dye – 'Pot 3'.
- Spoon about one third of 'Pot 3' into another pot – how much you'll need will depend on the size of the piece you're working on and the design you're printing. For example, a very 'open' design with lots of space for the dye to print through will need more dye paint than a more delicate design. Don't sweat the amounts too much and don't get twitchy about having to match the dye if you run out – approximates are okay!
- Add the equivalent amount of print paste to the dye paint in 'Pot 2' and stir well – you've now halved the strength or value of the dye. Give this pot a label by writing '2' on a piece of masking tape and stick it to the pot.
- Now take one third of the paint in 'Pot 2' and put it in yet another pot. Add the equivalent amount of print paste and stir well – you've now made a paint mixture that's a quarter of the strength of the original mixture. Label this pot '1'.
- Start printing with Pot 1; the weakest value. Aim to print all over the cloth but don't worry too much about getting a perfectly even distribution – some variation can add interest. Remember to work off the edges. Don't worry about ghosting.
- Now print all over the cloth again, using Pot 2.
- Finish by printing a final layer using Pot 3.
- Batch your cloth for a minimum of 4 hours (ideally overnight), then rinse, dry and contemplate it. You should have made a good start to a background and can now think about how to move the piece forward.

Layering Colour(s)

This exercise has many variations and involves printing a background with two or three colours. Your colour choices are enormous, but some examples might include:

- *A single hue:* for example, you may want a background of blue, but that background can contain many different blues. You could print in Turquoise, followed by Royal Blue. You could print in Turquoise or Royal, and then use Black as the second blue. You could print in all three; Turquoise, Royal and Black.
- *Analogous colour scheme:* an analogous colour scheme has colours in it that are close to each other. For example, yellow and orange, orange and red, red and purple, purple and blue, blue and green, green and yellow.
- *Complementary colour scheme:* pick colours that are opposite to each other. For example: blue and orange, yellow and purple, red and green.
- *Triadic colour scheme:* here, you print with all three primaries (Red, Yellow and Blue), or all three Secondaries (Orange, Purple and Green).

Chose your colour scheme and mix the thickened dyes in your chosen range of colours. To print:

- Consider your colours and choose the one that's likely to be the most easily bullied by the other colours. For example, yellow tends to be more quickly adulterated than red (particularly if the red is magenta). So start with the yellow and move on to print the other colour(s). Alternatively, start with the colour that you wish to have the most dominance in the piece as you'll then be able to print other colours on top with due consideration.
- Print three to five layers, then batch the cloth. Rinse, iron and pin up to contemplate your next move.

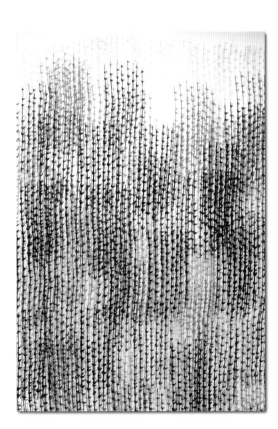

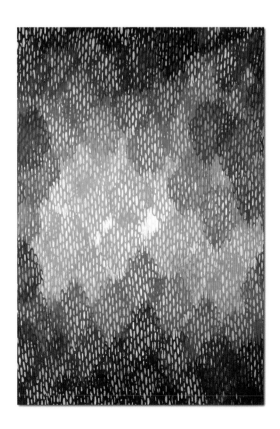

Layering Scale

The first two exercises will have enabled you to layer imagery as well as value and/or colour. This exercise allows you to explore perspective by layering the same design in three different sizes and three different values.

- Decide on an image (line or shape) and create that image for use with the screen in 3 different sizes: small, medium and large.
- Choose your cloth, scour, soda-soak and dry it before pinning it to the print surface.
- Mix a single colour of dye and then adjust it with print paste to achieve three values from dark to light (see page 77).
- Print the smallest image using the palest value of dye (Pot 1). Work all over the cloth, remembering to print off the edges.
- Now print the middle size image using the medium value dye paint (Pot 2). Work all over the cloth.
- Finish by printing the largest size in the darkest value (Pot 3).
- Batch, rinse and iron the piece before pinning it up to contemplate your next move.

Working with Sheers

Printing sheer fabric such as silk organza is a joy as it takes the dye paint so well. It's also useful to have sheers in your repetoire as they can work beautifully on top of other fabrics.

When you print a sheer, it's common for a fair amount of dye paint to go through the sheer, on to the drop cloth. Which means in no time at all your drop cloth can look splendid. Exploit this side-effect by putting silk organza or chiffon on top of another piece of 'good fabric; this could also be a sheer, or something of a heavier weight. Instead of dye paint being transferred on to your drop cloth, it'll go on to something potentially more worthwhile; resulting in a 'two'fer'; two fabrics being built through one process. The bottom layer may not be perfect, but will often be a good start.

Silk organza was laid on top of velvet before being printed with dye paints

5 different sizes of the same image were printed in various colours by Elaine Griffiths

WHAT NEXT?

Having generated background, where you go next is up to you, but do remember to think about the design considerations outlined on page 75. You could choose to continue building the background with your next move, or start to consider the placement of strong compositional elements. Have a dialogue with yourself and the cloth to help you move forward:

- Does the piece have a lot of texture? If so, is it time to consider introducing a shape, or strong lines?
- Does the piece contain a lot of line imagery? If so, is it time to consider introducing shape?
- Does the piece contain a lot of 'block' imagery or shapes? If so, is it time to introduce texture or line?
- Are there a lot of solid areas of colour? If so, is it time to introduce texture?
- Does the piece have a strong horizontal feel? If so, do you wish to build on this by perhaps introducing a strong horizon line, or would it be worth introducing a vertical element?
- Does the piece have a strong vertical feel? If so, do you wish to build on this by perhaps introducing a pathway or strong vertical line, or would it be worth introducing a horizontal element?
- Are all the angles at 90 or 180 degrees to each other? If so, what would introducing angular elements do?
- If you've been focused on building background, you may have a strong 'crystallographic' (all over) balance. Do you want to change that and create asymmetry, symmetry or a radial (central point – think Mandala) balance?
- Do you want to create a 'doorway into the picture world' by creating a focal point, pathway (straight, drifting or wiggly?) or horizon line (straight or undulating, low, middle or high?)
- The addition of a new image will drive contrast and visual interest, but if that image is of the same scale, and printed in a close colour and/or value, you'll probably continue to build background, which could be what you want at this stage. Or you, could consider sticking to the same image to build relationship, and drive contrast by…

  - → Manipulating the scale or size of the new or existing imagery (much bigger or much smaller)…
  - → Printing it in a different colour, or…
  - → Printing it in a different value: print darker or discharge to create lighter areas, or…
  - → Printing it in opaque or metallic paint to drive a strong sense of being on top/strongly foreground.

The possibilities are endless, which we acknowledge can be exciting and daunting at the same time. The only way to move forward is to move forward. Don't sit and cogitate forever or you'll stagnate. Just do something and learn from the results, accepting that not everything you do will turn out great… but it will turn out learning. And worst case scenario? Try:

- Re-scaling the piece (e.g. fold over the side(s), top and/or bottom).
- Look for small 'gems': cut out sections that work and move these on through more wet work or stitch.
- Over-dyeing; chuck the piece into a fairly strong bucket of dye. If you have no idea what colour to use, try either Black or a Red mixed from 1 part Scarlet (warm red), quarter part Magenta (cold red) and maybe a smidge of Brown.
- Cut it up and use it for quilt making or embroidery.
- Photograph it and make notes on where you went wrong/ why it's not right, then burn it in a ceremonial fashion.

Either way, enjoy your journey and keep learning.

Leslie is working compositionally using changes in value, colour and scale. She's also building a doorway into the piece through the use of a void/more open area

Resources/Suppliers

The website (www.committedtocloth.com) has a list of suppliers, but the following companies will be able to provide you with what you need. Remember, if it's a web-based company, many ship worldwide.

EUROPE

Art Van Go
The Studios, 1 Stevenage Road, Knebworth, Herts G3 6AN
www.artvango.co.uk

Atlantis Art
7-9 Plumber's Road, London E1 1EQ
www.atlantisart.co.uk

The Bramble Patch
West Street, Weedon, Northamptonshire NN7 4QU
www.thebramblepatch.co.uk

Fibrecrafts/George Weil
Old Portsmouth Road, Peasmarsh, Guildford, Surrey GU3 1LZ
www.fibrecrafts.co.uk

Great Art (web-based)
www.greatart.co.uk

Jacksons Art Supplies
Arch 66, Station Approach, Fulham, London SW6 3U
1 Farleigh Place, London N16 7SX
www.jacksonsart.co.uk

Quilt und Textile
Sebastiansplatz 4, Munich 80331, Germany
www.quiltundtextilkunst.de

Patchwork Shop
www.patchworhshop.de or www.pdpm.de

Thermofax Screens
Foxley Farm, Foxley, Towcester NN12 8HP
www.thermofaxscreens.co.uk

Whaleys
Harris Court, Great Horton, Bradford, West Yorkshire
www.whaleys-bradford.ltd.uk

Winifred Cottage
17 Elms Road, Fleet, Hampshire GU51 3EG
www.winifredcottage.co.uk

Zijdelings
Kapelstraat 93a, 5046 CL Tilberg, The Netherlands
www.zijdelings.com

NORTH AMERICA

Art Cloth Studios (U.S.A.)
www.artclothstudios.com

Dick Blick (U.S.A.)
PO Box 1267, Galesburgh, IL 61402
www.dickblick.com

Dharma Trading Company (U.S.A.)
1604 Fourth Street, San Rafael, California 94901
www.dharmatrading.com

GS Dye (Canada)
250 Dundas Street West, No. 8, Toronto M5T 2Z5, Ontario
www.gsdye.com

Jerry's Artarama (U.S.A.)
www.jerrysartarama.com

Maiwa (Canada)
6-1666 Johnston Street, Granville Island, Vancouver V6H 3SZ, B.C.
Maiwa.com

ProChemical & Dye (U.S.A.)
PO Box 14, Somerset, MA 02726
www.prochemical.com

Rupert, Gibbon & Spider (U.S.A.)
PO Box 452, Healdsburg, CA 95448
www.jacquardproducts.com

The Art Store (U.S.A.)
801 73rd Street, Windsor Heights, IA 5-312
www.shoptheartstore.com

NEW ZEALAND & AUSTRALIA

Artbeat of Tasmania (Tasmania, Australia)
85 Channel Highway, Kingston, Tasmania 7050
www.artbeattas.com

Batik Oetoro (Australia)
8/9 Arnhem Close, Gateshead, NSW 2290
www.dyeman.com

Essential Textile Art (Australia)
PO Box 3416, Rundle Mall, SA 5000
www.essentialtextileart.com

KraftKolour (Australia)
Box 379, Whittlesea, Victoria 3757
www.kraftkolour.com.au

New Zealand Quilter (New Zealand)
PO Box 14567, Kilbirnie, Wellington 6241
www.nzquilter.co.nz

The Thread Studio (Australia)
6 Smith Street, Perth 6000
www.thethreadstudio.com